Mindfulness-Based Cognitive Therapy

Mindfulness-Based Cognitive Therapy (MBCT) is increasingly used in therapeutic practice. It encourages clients to process experience without judgement as it arises, helping them to change their relationship with challenging thoughts and feelings, and accept that, even though difficult things may happen, it is possible to work with these in new ways.

This book provides a basis for understanding the key theoretical and practical features of MBCT. Focusing on a mindfulness-based cognitive therapy programme that is offered in a group context to those who are vulnerable to depressive relapses, the text is divided into 30 distinctive features that characterise the approach.

Mindfulness-Based Cognitive Therapy: Distinctive Features provides a concise, straightforward summary for professionals and trainees in the field. Its easy-to-use format will appeal to both experienced practitioners and newcomers with an interest in MBCT.

Rebecca Crane is an MBCT teacher and trainer and a Research Fellow within the Centre for Mindfulness Research and Practice, School of Psychology, Bangor University, UK.

Cognitive behavioural therapy (CBT) occupies a central position in the move towards evidence-based practice and is frequently used in the clinical environment. Yet there is no one universal approach to CBT and clinicians speak of first-, second-, and even third-wave approaches.

This series provides straightforward, accessible guides to a number of CBT methods, clarifying the distinctive features of each approach. The series editor, Windy Dryden, successfully brings together experts from each discipline to summarise the 30 main aspects of their approach divided into theoretical and practical features.

The CBT Distinctive Features Series will be essential reading for psychotherapists, counsellors, and psychologists of all orientations who want to learn more about the range of new and developing cognitive-behavioural approaches.

Titles in the series:

For further information about this series please visit
www.routledgementalhealth.com/cbt-distinctive-features

Mindfulness-Based Cognitive Therapy

Distinctive Features

Rebecca Crane

Routledge
Taylor & Francis Group

LONDON AND NEW YORK

First published 2009 by Routledge
27 Church Road, Hove, East Sussex BN3 2FA

Simultaneously published in the USA and Canada
by Routledge
270 Madison Avenue, New York NY 10016

Reprinted 2009 (twice) and 2010 (three times)

*Routledge is an imprint of the Taylor & Francis Group,
an Informa business*

Typeset in Times by Garfield Morgan,
Swansea, West Glamorgan
Printed and bound in Great Britain by
TJ International Ltd, Padstow, Cornwall

This publication has been produced with paper manufactured to
strict environmental standards and with pulp derived from
sustainable forests.

British Library Cataloguing in Publication Data
A catalogue record for this book is available from the British Library

Library of Congress Cataloging in Publication Data
Crane, Rebecca, 1964–
   Mindfulness-based cognitive therapy : distinctive features /
Rebecca Crane.
       p. ; cm.
   Includes bibliographical references and index.
   ISBN 978-0-415-44501-6 (hardback : alk. paper) –
   ISBN 978-0-415-44502-3 (pbk. : alk. paper) 1. Mindfulness-based
cognitive therapy. I. Title.
   [DNLM: 1. Cognitive Therapy–methods. 2. Depressive Disorder–
therapy. 3. Mind–Body and Relaxation Techniques.
WM 425.5.C6 C891m 2009]
   RC489.M55C73 2009
   616.89'142–dc22
                                                   2008017140

ISBN: 978-0–415–44501–6 (hbk)
ISBN: 978-0–415–44502–3 (pbk)

Dedicated to the potential in each of us moment by moment to be free from suffering, and to the endeavour to realise this.

Contents

Acknowledgements

I am reminded as I write these acknowledgements of how all that we do is interconnected with those around us. I feel deeply appreciative of the myriad of relationships and influences that have directly and indirectly been a part of my learning and have made this book possible.

In developing my understanding of mindfulness practice and of the teaching of Mindfulness-Based Cognitive Therapy, I have been profoundly blessed with inspirational teachers and friends. First and foremost I am forever grateful to Mark Williams. He has been a generous and steady presence, an ongoing teacher, colleague, friend, and mentor throughout this learning process. My friendship and connection with Ferris Urbanowski, and the teaching she has given over the years, has enlivened my sense of what is possible and has been profoundly significant to me. I am deeply grateful to the many other teachers who have inspired me, in particular Melissa Blacker, Jon Kabat-Zinn and Christina Feldman. The friendship, shared teaching ventures, and explorations I enjoy with Pamela Erdmann, David Elias and Trish Bartley have been particularly significant contributors to my journey.

Profound gratitude to Mark Williams, John Teasdale, Ferris Urbanowski, Trish Bartley, David Elias, Pamela Erdmann, Susan Woods and Windy Dryden for giving their time to reading drafts of this writing and offering feedback and suggestions. Their engagement and support in gradually refining how to articulate what is being expressed here has been invaluable.

I am deeply grateful for my ongoing participation and collaboration with the Centre for Mindfulness Research and Practice teaching group—David Elias, Trish Bartley, Judith Soulsby, Sarah Silverton, Jody Mardulla, Cindy Cooper, Michael Chaskalson, Eluned Gold, Annee Griffiths and Vanessa Hope. Much of the learning that is on these pages has been gathered through their gentle and determined presence, which has supported me in learning ways to bring mindfulness to the heart of my life and work and through the engaged and passionate explorations that take place between us. I also want to express my gratitude to Caroline Creasey, Anne Douglas and Sue Griffiths who create a dependable and good hearted organisational bedrock for my work within the Centre for Mindfulness Research and Practice, and who also offer an invaluable contribution to unfolding the vision we have for our work. Thank you dear friends.

Within Bangor University, I would like to extend my appreciation to Ian Russell, who for many years created the conditions within which the Centre for Mindfulness Research and Practice could develop and who encouraged me to take on this particular writing project.

In representing this work I am aware that I am offering out a small drop within a long and rich lineage of teaching and learning. I am deeply grateful to all who have contributed to this stream of learning—in particular to Jon Kabat-Zinn, Saki Santorelli and to all their colleagues at the Center for Mindfulness in Massachusetts, USA who developed Mindfulness-Based Stress Reduction; to Zindel Segal, John Teasdale and Mark Williams who developed Mindfulness-Based Cognitive Therapy; to participants and students of mindfulness-based courses and training programmes throughout the world and to the many people who have been a part of this collective learning whom I do not know.

All my work takes place within the context of a full and rich family life. Thank you to my husband Mark for his steady, loving support. Thank you to my children Joel, Ellie and Freya for their love of life and for keeping me awake and alive to what is truly important.

Permission acknowledgements

Grateful acknowledgement is made to the following for permission to reprint previously published material:

"The body is happy (like any other living being) when we pay kindly attention to it" from a talk on scanning the body by Ajahn Sumedho (2006), reprinted with permission of the English Sangha Trust.

Excerpts from *Coming to Our Senses: Healing Ourselves and the World Through Mindfulness* by Jon Kabat-Zinn. Copyright © 2005 Jon Kabat-Zinn, PhD. Reprinted by permission of Hyperion. All rights reserved.

Excerpt from *Sunbathing in the Rain: A Cheerful Book on Depression* by Gwyneth Lewis. Copyright © 2002 Gwyneth Lewis. Reproduced by permission of HarperCollins Publishers Ltd and Jessica Kingsley Publishers.

Excerpts from *Mindfulness Meditation for Everyday Life* by Jon Kabat-Zinn, 1994. Reprinted with permission of Little Brown Book Group and Abner Stein.

Excerpts from *The Essential Rumi* translated by Coleman Barks with John Moyne, A. J. Arberry and Reynold Nicholson (Penguin Books 1999). Copyright © Coleman Barks, 1995.

Reprinted with permission of Penguin Group (UK) and HarperOne, a division of HarperCollins USA.

Meditation quote from page 105 of Melissa Blacker (2002) "Meditation", in M. A. Bright (ed.), *Holistic Health and Healing*. Reprinted by permission of F. A. Davis Company.

Quote from Saki Santorelli (1999) *Heal Thyself: Lessons on Mindfulness in Medicine*. New York: Bell Tower. Reproduced by Permission of Random House Inc.

Note

Throughout this book the names of clients in the case study notes have been changed for the sake of anonymity.

Foreword

"I couldn't believe it at first; then others said the same thing."

It was a bright lunchtime on an unseasonably warm Tuesday in January, 2008. We were sitting around a coffee table in the Common Room in Oxford University's Department of Psychiatry. The speaker was a distinguished professor of psychiatry in Oxford, an international expert on the most serious of mood disorders.

"I have referred hundreds of people for psychological treatment over the years, but I have never seen responses like this."

He was talking of a number of his patients with diagnoses of depression and bipolar disorder (manic depression) who had recently completed a programme of mindfulness-based cognitive therapy (MBCT). Each had been referred to our Oxford MBCT classes because they had found themselves having suicidal thoughts and plans whenever they got depressed; many had attempted suicide in the past or come very close to it.

"What is it you noticed about them?" I asked.

"Well, it's difficult to describe. They say that they have never felt better, that they have found a way of dealing with their difficulties that is completely different from anything else they have ever come across. At first I wondered if they were becoming manic again; but no; they were saying that something had completely transformed their lives. And it was not just one who said this; many others said the same."

I found myself being naturally cautious. After all, this had only been a pilot programme, part of our efforts gradually to extend the application of mindfulness-based approaches to the most challenging of mental health difficulties. We still did not know if these immediate changes would translate into lasting prevention of relapse for people with these diagnoses. And yet . . . this was not the first time that I had heard these sorts of comments. They fitted with many others—mental health experts and their patients—who have found things changing in unexpected ways by the experience of intensive practice in meditative disciplines.

It is a far cry from the early days when, 15 years before, Zindel Segal, John Teasdale and I went to see Jon Kabat-Zinn and his colleagues at the UMass Medical Center in Worcester, MA. As we tell in the book we wrote for clinicians (Segal, Williams, & Teasdale, 2002), at that time we differed between us in our attitude to what we would likely discover, and our first visit did not resolve these many doubts. For myself, I was pretty sure that this was the wrong approach to depression. First, even if we learned the practice of mindfulness meditation, and even if our research found that it had something to offer our recurrently depressed patients, how could we expect our colleagues to commit to a practice of mindfulness meditation in order to be in a position to teach it to others? "Just do the maths", I said. "At best, the practice of mindfulness in a healthcare setting is going to end up as a minority activity, staying for ever on the fringes of what could be offered to patients."

My second set of doubts was even more fundamental. Having never meditated myself prior to this meeting, I assumed (looking from the outside) that what was being taught in class was just another form of relaxation, and we already had evidence that relaxation training was not effective in depression.

Although we committed to the personal practice of mindfulness meditation, I remained sceptical.

It turned out that I was spectacularly wrong. Yes, we were able to show that MBCT is effective in reducing relapse and recurrence in those who have experienced repeated episodes of depression, but I was wrong about everything else. The enthusiasm of clinicians for learning to cultivate mindfulness in their own lives in order to teach it to others has been extraordinary. Indeed, it has far outstripped the current evidence base, which, although it is expanding, is doing so at the usual slow rate characteristic of the most serious and important scientific endeavours.

I was also wrong about what mindfulness is. I found my scepticism dissolving as I began to witness, again and again, the power of this approach to transform lives. For one thing, from inside the practice of mindfulness meditation, it becomes clear that meditation is very different from relaxation. Nor indeed is it, in its essence, a form of psychotherapy, as we normally understand it, at all.

It is all very well to say what it is not. It is much more difficult to say what it is. This is where this wonderful book by Rebecca Crane comes in.

Becca has directed Bangor University's Centre for Mindfulness Research and Practice for many years, helping it to become the leading centre in Europe for training in mindfulness-based approaches in physical and mental healthcare. Working closely with colleagues in the UK and from the Center for Mindfulness in Medicine, Healthcare and Society at UMass (now directed by Dr Saki Santorelli), Becca and her colleagues have extensive experience in offering mindfulness classes to many hundreds of people with physical and emotional challenges, and have carefully and with great wisdom developed a comprehensive programme of training for those wishing to teach mindfulness to others. She is in a unique position to write this book, as both a participant and observer of the recent developments in the field, nationally and internationally.

And here it is: a clear account of what MBCT is, both in its theoretical perspectives and its actual practices. Written in accessible language, it is an extraordinary achievement that will be highly valued by both participants in mindfulness classes and their teachers. Thank you, Becca, for writing it.

Mark Williams
Oxford, February 2008

Introduction

The intention of this book is to concisely lay out the distinctive features of Mindfulness-Based Cognitive Therapy (MBCT). My hope is that it serves as a basis for understanding the key theoretical and practical features of MBCT and becomes a basis for further exploration. By definition it is incomplete. The risk of articulating such a complex and multidimensional approach in a concise and structured way is that this might be perceived as the whole picture—which is far from the case.

It is particularly challenging to articulate theory in relation to mindfulness practice and many longer term practitioners and teachers would smile at attempts to do so! One teacher likened this to trying to pin jelly to the wall! Mindfulness practice and teaching are pointing us towards subtle, profound and indefinable characteristics of the mind that go way beyond easy psychological description. The endeavour to articulate the processes that we believe to be in action when we practice mindfulness is thus inherent with paradox and could be seen as reductive. However, incomplete as it may be, it is useful to work to clarify and articulate our understandings—so long as we hold in mind all that we don't know as we do this! I ask you to remember this as you read. This book may convey the impression that the theory is more defined and solid than it really is.

The parents of MBCT are Mindfulness-Based Stress Reduction, which itself draws from the 2500 year legacy of mindfulness teaching within its Buddhist context, and also from cognitive-behavioural scientific and therapeutic principles. Those who want to go more deeply into their understanding of MBCT will need to give space and time to an exploration of these areas that gave rise to it. There is a wealth of resources that can support this, some of which are cited at the end of the book.

The opportunity to write this book came to me through my work as a teacher and trainer within the Centre for Mindfulness Research and Practice, Bangor University. I have been privileged to play a central role in the development of this centre over the last six years, along with the colleagues and friends who form the teaching group and the administrative team. Founded by Professor Mark Williams, while he led the Bangor arm of the first research trial of MBCT, the centre gathered together the expertise and interest that had formed during this time. As an occupational therapist engaged in offering one-to-one and group therapy within a local community mental health team, this research trial on my doorstep caught my professional interest. The personal pull was equally strong. Through an interest that arose during my student years, supported by a range of wonderful teachers and retreat periods, I had a personal mindfulness practice—a deeply important bedrock within my life. Although mindfulness practice was central in informing my personal process while I was engaged in therapy with clients, it was not an explicit part of my work. The possibility of joining the threads of my life was compelling.

Mindfulness practice and teaching reminds us that the personal and the universal are forever entwined. For me this time of developing mindfulness-based training programmes within the Centre for Mindfulness Research and Practice has taken place while my children were in their youngest years, with all the turbulence, wonder and celebration that this time holds for many of us. One of the gifts of teaching mindfulness within our professional lives is the "wake up call" it brings to us to hold an intention to live the approach as fully as we are able in our personal lives. The (often challenging) reality check that my family has offered to me has been an invaluable teaching! Similarly, as a group of teachers, we hold an ongoing intention to apply the same rigour to our personal and group development, as we bring to the development of our training programmes. More than at any other period in my life, I have discovered in these years that this intention to live as consciously as we are able within the detail of our lives, is the food that nourishes our explorations and understanding in a wider sense.

It is an exciting time to be engaged in this work. There is an upsurge of interest and development at the interface of contemplative traditions and psychology: a growing sense of the potential for mindfulness within therapeutic settings. However, the current evidence base for MBCT is still quite small. Juxtaposed alongside this is wide interest in and enthusiasm for its potential—a potential that is equally relevant to the professionals as it is to their clients and patients. Although many become interested in mindfulness because of the hope it seems to offer to their clients, they soon find that it isn't possible to discover the approach other than through a very personal engagement with it. Most experience this engagement as challenging but also tremendously rewarding—"The practice has helped me to see my life through new eyes"; "I feel nourished in ways which go way beyond the immediate relevance of this to my clinical practice". The experience and practice of mindfulness may be challenging to describe, yet when it touches us it does so in ways that fundamentally change our orientation to ourselves and the world.

This book focuses on a particular expression of the current interest in the integration of mindfulness and therapeutic approaches: the MBCT programme offered in a group context for people with a particular clinical problem—vulnerability to depressive relapse. There are of course many other skilful means to offer mindfulness-based approaches in therapeutic settings—although this book might inform these it does not specifically address them. The main evidence base for MBCT is currently in relation to its effects for people with recurrent depression. There are, however, other targeted versions of MBCT being developed, researched and used in clinical practice, including MBCT for the recurrence of suicidal depression, for chronic fatigue syndrome, for oncology patients, for anxiety disorders and for general stress reduction. Many of the psychological processes described in this book will be relevant to these other populations but not all. Given the broader evidence base for Mindfulness-Based Stress Reduction (MBSR), which demonstrates positive effect sizes for a range of conditions, there is good support for these developments. At this early stage in the development of mindfulness-based applications, there is, though, a gap between the evidence base and the promise that the approach appears to hold. In the important process of extending the use of MBCT to different client populations and into new contexts, it is important to hold in mind what we do not know and to proceed into new territory with caution and care.

This book, in line with others in this series, is divided into 15 Points on the distinctive theoretical features and 15 Points on the distinctive practical features of MBCT. Given the similarity between MBCT and MBSR there are a range of features that are distinctive to both approaches. In these instances the generic label "mindfulness-based approach" or the "eight-week mindfulness-based programme" is used. The theory that this book primarily focuses on is the cognitive scientific background to the work. There is also reference to the Buddhist underpinning to mindfulness. There are other theoretical frameworks that usefully contribute to the understanding of the teaching process in MBCT (in particular learning theory and group theory), which are not given space here.

Writing this has been a rich learning experience for me. I hope that it contributes to your learning and in turn informs the lives of the people with whom you work.

Rebecca Crane
March 2008

Abbreviations used

MBCT: Mindfulness-Based Cognitive Therapy
MBSR: Mindfulness-Based Stress Reduction
CBT: Cognitive Behavioural Therapy
TAU: Treatment As Usual
3MBS: Three Minute Breathing Space

Part 1

THE DISTINCTIVE THEORETICAL FEATURES OF MBCT

1

An integration of Mindfulness-Based Stress Reduction and Cognitive Behavioural Therapy

Mindfulness-Based Cognitive Therapy (MBCT) was developed as a targeted approach for people who have a history of depression and are therefore vulnerable to future episodes. Taught while participants are in remission, it aims to enable them to learn how to bring awareness to body sensations, thoughts, and emotions and to respond adaptively to the early warning signs of relapse. The programme has the practice of mindfulness meditation at its core; it draws on the structure and process of the Mindfulness-Based Stress Reduction (MBSR) programme and integrates within these some aspects of Cognitive Behavioural Therapy (CBT) for depression. It is taught in an eight-week class format for up to twelve participants. This Point offers a summary of these areas which are integral to MBCT and have informed its development: mindfulness meditation practice, MBSR and CBT.

Mindfulness

Mindfulness is an aspect of a number of ancient spiritual traditions. Within the tradition of Buddhism it is an integral part of the path towards understanding the origins and cessation of suffering; and it is a means to free oneself from the pattern of adding suffering to existing difficulty and pain (Gunaratana, 2002). Mindfulness thus enables us to see and work with the universal vulnerabilities and challenges that are an inherent part of being human. Mindful awareness is neither religious nor esoteric in its nature and is potentially accessible and applicable

3

to all (Grossman, Niemann, Schmidt, & Walach, 2004; Kabat-Zinn, 2003).

Mindfulness is the awareness that emerges when we pay attention to experience in a particular way: on purpose (the attention is deliberately placed on particular aspects of experience); in the present moment (when the mind slips into the past or the future we bring it back to the present); and non-judgementally (the process is infused with a spirit of acceptance of whatever arises) (Kabat-Zinn, 1994). It is simply being aware of what is going on, as it is arising, attending deeply and directly with it and relating to it with acceptance: a powerful act of participatory observation. Although simple in its intention and essence, mindfulness practice often feels hard work. It is a practice through which we systematically train ourselves to be confident to "turn towards" whatever arises in our experience. This runs counter to our instinct to avoid the difficult and challenging aspects to our experience.

Mindfulness teaching and practice contains three broad elements:

1 *The development of awareness* through a systematic methodology involving formal mindfulness practices (body scan, sitting meditation, mindful movement) and informal mindfulness practice (cultivating present-moment awareness in daily life).

2 *A particular attitudinal framework* characterised by kindness, curiosity, and a willingness to be present with the unfolding of experience. These attitudes are both deliberately cultivated within the practice and emerge spontaneously from it.

3 *An embodied understanding of human vulnerability.* This is developed through hearing teachings, and then exploring their validity through directly seeing our experiential process in action during mindfulness meditation practice. We learn through this that although suffering is an inherent part of our experience, there are ways that we can learn to recognise and step out of the patterns of habitually

collaborating to perpetuate it, add to it and deepen it. Within its original Buddhist context, mindfulness is taught as a key part of an integrated system, which supports us in recognising the nature of human suffering and in working consciously with it as it arises for ourselves.

Brought together, these elements of mindfulness teaching and practice offer the potential for us to develop insight, new perspectives, and so to facilitate personal transformation.

In taking mindfulness out of its original Buddhist context and recontextualising it within a secular programme such as MBCT or MBSR, it is important to ensure that the critical aspects of the approach that bring about change are not lost (Teasdale, Segal, & Williams, 2003). This is a complex question with many elements to it, including the issue of the specific teacher qualities required by the nature of the MBCT learning process (discussed in Point 30). The aspect of this addressed here is the ingredients of the programme itself. The three broad elements of mindfulness practice outlined above are mirrored in the construction of the secular eight-session programme. So, an MBCT programme contains:

1 *The cultivation of awareness* through mindfulness practice.
2 *A particular attitudinal framework* characterised by non-striving, acceptance, and a genuine interest in experience. This is largely conveyed implicitly through the teaching process, which is infused with these qualities.
3 *A process of linking the learning to an understanding of working with vulnerability*. The personal experiential learning is integrated within a wider framework of understanding. This understanding relates both to the nature of general human vulnerability and suffering and to the particular nature of vulnerability to depressive relapse. During the MBCT sessions this integration is facilitated through dialogue, reflection, group exercises, and teaching.

The three developers of MBCT—Zindel Segal, of the Center for Addiction and Mental Health (Clark Division) in Toronto, Mark Williams, then of the University of Wales, Bangor, and John Teasdale, then of the Applied Psychology Unit of the Medical Research Council in Cambridge—commenced their development process by first reviewing a theoretical understanding of the basis of vulnerability to depressive relapse and recurrence.[1] This led them to the recognition that a key protective mechanism in preventing depressive relapse is the ability to "de-centre" or step back from our thought processes. Through the particular experience of one of the developers, the understanding emerged that this, and other skills relevant to the prevention of depression, can be developed through mindfulness meditation practice. Segal, Williams, and Teasdale (2002) were thus led to the work of Jon Kabat-Zinn.

Mindfulness-Based Stress Reduction

Kabat-Zinn (1990) pioneered the integration of traditional Buddhist mindfulness meditation practices into an accessible psycho-educational eight-session programme called Mindfulness-Based Stress Reduction (MBSR). Kabat-Zinn's intention and vision in developing MBSR was to render the learning from the ancient practice of mindfulness into an accessible, secular, and mainstream programme, which could inform the lives of patients who suffer from chronic pain and a variety of other conditions. Mindfulness was thus recontextualised and taught in a group-based, secular, educational programme and integrated with psychological understanding, models of stress from mind-body medicine, and explorations on working with the

---

1 Although relapse and recurrence have slightly different meanings, for simplicity the term relapse will be used hereon. The term relapse refers to the continuation of a single episode of depression, which has been masked by the person taking antidepressants, while the term recurrence refers to the commencement of a completely new episode of depression (Kupfer, 1991).

challenges of modern living. The programme thus involves intensive training in mindfulness meditation, and teaching which enables participants to apply the learning from the practices into the practicalities of the management of challenge within daily life.

The MBSR programme was originally taught to groups of participants with a range of physical and psychological challenges and has now also been adapted to a variety of specific diagnoses and conditions. These include patients with diagnoses such as cancer, rheumatic conditions and eating disorders, and contexts such as prisons, low-income inner-city areas, medical education and corporate settings. In the United States MBSR has become a part of a newly recognised field of integrative medicine.

The overall way the programmes are structured into eight weekly psycho-educational style sessions, and the sequencing of the introduction of the different mindfulness practices, is similar in MBCT and in MBSR. The core difference is the way the programme learning is shaped towards the participants that it is designed for.

Cognitive Behavioural Therapy

The CBT contribution within the MBCT integration takes two broad forms:

1   It offers an underpinning cognitive framework and understanding drawn from CBT for depression (Beck, Rush, Shaw, & Emery, 1979). This informed the development of the approach (see Point 2) and informs the teaching process through offering an understanding that enables the teacher and the participants to link the learning to depression (see Point 14).
2   It informs the inclusion of curriculum elements drawn from CBT (see Point 27).

Summary

Mindfulness meditation is the foundation of the MBCT programme; MBSR informs its structure, content and teaching style; and aspects of CBT for depression inform some content and elements of the teaching process.

2

Underpinned by the cognitive theory of vulnerability to depression

It is estimated by the World Health Organization that by the year 2020 unipolar major depression will be the disease imposing the second greatest burden of ill health worldwide (Murray & Lopez, 1996), very close behind the top cause, ischaemic heart disease. A key feature of major depression is the likelihood that sufferers will experience repeated episodes. It follows, therefore, that the heightened vulnerability to relapse for people with a history of depression is the aspect of the problem that needs particular attention, if the personal and global impact of it are to be lessened.

Developing a cost-effective relapse-prevention approach

Prior to the development of MBCT the most evidence-based strategies for preventing depressive relapse were:

- *Maintenance pharmacotherapy*—this is the most widely used strategy for preventing depressive relapse (Kupfer et al., 1992) but its preventative effect lasts only as long as the medication is being taken.
- *Cognitive Behavioural Therapy*—research indicates that people who have had CBT during depression are less prone to relapse than those who have not (e.g. Hollon et al., 2005).

While it is encouraging that antidepressant medication is effective in treating acute depressive episodes, and that CBT is effective both during an episode *and* in preventing future episodes, there are disadvantages to both these treatments. Patients taking maintenance pharmacotherapy need to keep taking it for a long time for the beneficial effect to be sustained. CBT relies on the person engaging one-to-one with a skilled, scarce and expensive therapist. The aim of the three MBCT developers, therefore, was to develop a relapse-prevention approach which could be delivered:

1   In a group format. (The high prevalence of depression, along with the cost of one-to-one therapy, creates the need for approaches dealing with the problem to be cost effective if they are to become more widely available.)
2   While the participants are in remission (having gener-ally recovered through treatment with antidepressant medication).

In setting out to develop a new approach to preventing depressive relapse, Segal, Teasdale, and Williams first spent time coming to understand more fully the ways in which this particular vulnerability is created and maintained, and the particular processes of mind that may reverse it. Essentially, they were asking two questions: first, "What is the basis for the increased vulnerability to depressive relapse?" and, second, "What are the skills developed through CBT during an episode of depression which reduce the longer term vulnerability to relapse?" (Teasdale, 2006).

Vulnerability to depressive relapse

As a person experiences more episodes of depression less environmental stress is required to provoke another episode. This is because their internal style of thinking and experiencing has developed into a particular pattern, which creates and perpetuates itself (Post, 1992). So, what is creating this increasing vulnerability to future depression with each episode?

It is a normal part of the pattern of everyone's life to experience episodes and phases of lowered moods. For people who have experienced depression in the past, these moments of occurrence of lowered mood are moments of heightened vulnerability to depressive relapse. Two linked factors make mild sadness more likely to persist and deepen: rumination and experiential avoidance:

- *Rumination* is a particular style of self-critical, self-focused, repetitive, negative thinking. It is preoccupied with and driven by the desire to "solve" the emotional challenge of unhappiness or lowered mood (see Point 6 for more on rumination).
- *Experiential avoidance* is the attempt to remain out of contact with the direct experience of challenging thoughts, emotions and body sensations (see Point 7 for more on experiential avoidance).

The experience of depression comes as a constellation and interaction of lowered mood, ruminative thinking patterns, experiential avoidance and physical sensations of fatigue and heaviness. During episodes of depression the association between these elements is formed and learned. Repeated episodes of depression strengthen the learnt associations between the components and leave an imprint of memory in the cognitive, emotional and physical patterning of the person, which remains generally unseen but poised to be reactivated at times of low mood. This means that during periods of remission a small lowering of mood can have the effect of retriggering the patterns that are associated with previous sad moods. This process, named "differential activation", is a key way through which depressive relapse is triggered (Teasdale, 1988; Teasdale, Segal, & Williams, 2000).

How does Cognitive Behavioural Therapy reduce the risk of relapse?

It was important to the MBCT developers to understand *what* is helping to protect people who have engaged in CBT during a depression episode from future relapse. The relapse-prevention approach they were developing could usefully seek to develop these same skills.

Detailed theoretical analysis led to this hypothesis: the effect of repeatedly working with the content of thoughts and with habitual avoidant tendencies during CBT is to gradually create a shift in the client's overall perspective in *relationship* to their thoughts and emotions. Through a process of engagement with CBT, the client comes to perceive that challenging thoughts and emotions are passing events in the mind that do not necessarily reflect reality and are not central components of the self (Segal et al., 2002). This altered, "de-centred" relationship or stance towards thoughts and emotions is significant. It is this that creates the person's ability to step out of the entanglement of ruminative thinking and the consequences of low mood cycles.

Therefore, although not a direct target of CBT, this "de-centred" relationship to thoughts arises implicitly during the learning process. By contrast, developing the skill to "de-centre" from one's experience is an *explicit* and deliberate intention of the MBCT learning process. Consequently, there is no emphasis in MBCT, as there is in conventional CBT, on changing belief in the content of thoughts. The focus is on a systematic training to be more aware, moment by moment, of physical sensations, thoughts and emotions as events in the field of awareness. This gradually facilitates the potential to develop this "de-centred" relationship to thoughts, emotions and body sensations. We learn that we can see them as aspects of experience that move through our awareness rather than seeing them as reality. We learn to relate *to* the thinking process rather than *from* the content of thoughts themselves—we can see that our thoughts are not facts, they are just thoughts.

Summary

The three main areas that have been outlined in this Point are:

1 The nature of depression as a recurring condition.
2 The main psychological pattern that creates vulnerability to depressive relapse is the way in which a small amount of sad mood can trigger old habitual patterns of self-denigrating thinking, leading to repetitive cycles of ruminative thinking and experiential avoidance. Together these form a general pattern of processing experience, which although motivated by the wish to remove depression actually keeps it in place.
3 Developing a perspective which recognises that negative ruminative thoughts and low mood are aspects of experience rather than a central aspect of self (a "de-centred" perspective) is a key factor in conferring protection to those vulnerable to depressive relapse and recurrence.

3

Learning skills to reduce the risk of depressive relapse

The particular ways in which depression-prone people tend to process their experience creates both an increased vulnerability to relapse and, once depression is re-established, the factors that maintain it. The specific intention of MBCT is to provide participants with a means to work effectively with these processes at times of potential depressive relapse. Essentially mindfulness and "relapse-related" mind states are incompatible. The MBCT

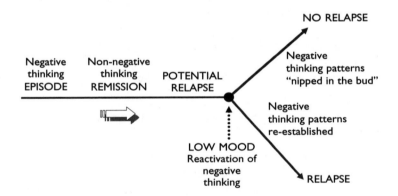

Figure 1 Model representing the cognitive risk of depressive relapse. The mindfulness-based cognitive therapy course is taken during remission and the skills developed are intended to take effect at the point of potential relapse. (Reproduced with permission from Segal, Z. V., Williams, J. M. G. and Teasdale, J. D. (2002). *Mindfulness-Based Cognitive Therapy for Depression: A New Approach to Preventing Relapse.* New York: Guilford Press.)

course is taken during a period of remission and the skills developed are intended to take effect at the point of potential relapse. Figure 1 offers a diagrammatic representation of this.

So, how do the skills learnt on an MBCT course interface with the vulnerability of heightened risk of depressive relapse? The practice of mindfulness and the other curriculum elements of the MBCT programme have four broad learning intentions in relation to depressive relapse-inducing processes. Participants are learning to develop the potential to:

1   Step out of ruminative thinking patterns.
2   Recognise and be more aware of potential relapse-related mind-body processes.
3   Access new ways to relate to both depression-related and other aspects of experience.
4   Turn towards, befriend and engage with both difficult and other aspects of experience.

An overview of the significance of these four areas of learning is now given. Key learning themes in the eight-week MBCT course are highlighted in *italics* within this.

1 Learning to step out of ruminative thinking patterns

Our conscious attention is only able to process a limited amount of information over a given time. So, by deliberately paying attention to certain aspects of experience, we naturally exclude other aspects from our immediate attention and thus remove the resources that sustain them (Teasdale, Segal, & Williams, 1995). Essentially therefore, *being with the actuality of the present moment through a deliberate focus on sensations in the body* redirects our attentional resources away from ruminative thinking. Rather than pursuing the urge to solve problems through the conceptual mind, the attention is taken to direct experience. Thoughts are simply acknowledged as events in the field of awareness. This serves to pre-empt the establishment of negative cycles (Teasdale et al., 1995). Through repeated practice of mindfulness skills, participants are training their internal processing mechanisms to create new "intentional habits", which arise through an awareness of moment-by-moment experience, rather than being driven by automatic and habitual patterns of internal processing. This new repertoire of responses becomes part of the person's store of memory (Teasdale et al., 1995) and so is more likely to be accessible when it is particularly needed during states of mild depression (i.e. *before* the patterns have consolidated into major depression).

2 Learning to recognise and be more aware of relapse-related modes of processing

The development of mindful awareness in MBCT is initially focused on illuminating and revealing to participants, through their own direct experience, the effects of habitual patterns of "mindlessness". In particular, participants are witnessing *the general patterns and habits of their mind*; and *the particular tendency to be on automatic pilot and caught up in ruminative thinking cycles*. Participants are enabled to see these patterns clearly. They become attuned to the ways in which they inadvertently collaborate to trigger and maintain both their general suffering and their tendency to become depressed.

3 Learning to access a new way to relate to both depression-related and other aspects of experience

The shift towards a more mindful mode of being, which involves both acceptance and paying attention to the actuality of the present moment, enables participants to access new ways to process or "be with" depression-related and other aspects of experience (Teasdale, 1999, 2006). As described in number 1 above, one effect of becoming mindful of the detail of physical sensations is that the "fuel" needed to maintain negative thoughts is withdrawn. A further effect of interrupting this habitual focus on negative thinking patterns is a movement towards a fresh "mode of mind". This opens the potential for us to relate to experience in a radically different way thus allowing new learning and perspectives to emerge. This can be described as a shift from "doing mode" into "being mode" (Segal et al., 2002).

This shift of "mind mode" enables participants to relate to existing experience from a different perspective—a "different place". This new way of seeing experience involves recognising that our experience is not necessarily what creates our identity. In this way difficulty arising in any aspect of our experience— physical pain, painful emotions or negative thoughts—can be seen as *an* aspect of our experience in *this* moment. This can create a shift in perception from seeing the difficulty as an all-encompassing experience, which eliminates awareness of everything else and which becomes the way we identify ourselves, to seeing it as part of the "tapestry" and flux of one's life. In this way it can become possible to take the difficulty less personally and to hold it more lightly. MBCT participants thus learn to *be able to relate to aspects of experience and ruminative thought patterns in particular from a "de-centred" perspective.* They learn that it is possible to relate *to* rather than *from* their experience. Rather than being lost and caught within the content of thoughts, it becomes possible to hold them in a wider perspective.

Another key aspect of operating from this new mode of mind—"being mode"—is that it enables participants to bring their direct moment-to-moment awareness to bear on their decisions and actions in life. Participants are thus enabled to *use mindful awareness as a place from which to make choices about taking appropriate action and about how to look after themselves wisely.* There is thus an explicit learning link made between "being with" and accepting the present moment, and then responding wisely to it.

4 Learning to turn towards, befriend and engage with both difficult and other aspects of experience

The fourth area of broad learning that is a key component of MBCT is the training in "turning towards" the range of experiences we have—pleasant, unpleasant and neutral. This can reverse or offer an alternative to the experiential avoidance of difficult emotions, which is known to be a key contributor to relapse. This ability to "turn towards" is cultivated through participants developing an interest and curiosity in the unfolding of their experience. Participants learn to infuse this stance of interest in their experience with qualities of warmth, kindness and compassion.

As described above, the first step taught in MBCT is always to pause and clearly see: participants thus learn to recognise *habitual patterns of avoiding difficult emotions*. They learn to bring to their experience and particularly to these difficult areas *an attitudinal framework characterised by acceptance, kindliness and curiosity towards their internal experience*. This enables participants to learn to taste a new way of relating to difficulty. From being habitually self-critical and judgemental they are invited in MBCT to bring an open, interested, warm, accepting and compassionate stance towards experience. This begins a shift from avoidant ways of processing experience to a deliberate "turning towards" experience.

Summary

MBCT participants are learning to recognise their "doing" mode of mind and to understand how it can create and perpetuate difficult mind states; they are learning to develop the capacity to engage with their "being" mode of mind and to cultivate the potential to approach emotional challenge through this. The aim of the Points that now follow is to tease out in more detail the elements of the MBCT programme that have been outlined in this Point.

4

The significance of automatic pilot

We may never be quite where we actually are, never quite in touch with the fullness of our possibilities.

(Jon Kabat-Zinn[2])

Most people spontaneously experience some moments of being fully engaged with present-moment experience without being caught up in thought-based formulations or concepts about it. For many though, a fog of preoccupations and preconceptions habitually clouds the present moment much of the time. The rationale for mindfulness being the foundation of MBCT rests on the skills, which a mindfulness practice confers, of enabling one to *intentionally* disengage from automatic pilot with its associated style of habitual ruminative thought processes; to bring the attention back to the actuality of the moment; and so to open the possibility of a wiser responsiveness to the situation. In this Point I aim to explore the state of mind that we call automatic pilot, some of its beneficial and harmful effects and the ways that it interfaces with the state of mindful awareness.

The term "automatic pilot" describes a state of mind in which one acts without conscious intention or awareness of present-moment sensory perception. The activity engaged in might be physical or mental but the key characteristic is that awareness of the present moment is clouded. The ability to operate on automatic pilot is highly developed in the human

2 Kabat-Zinn, 1994, *Mindfulness Meditation for Everyday Life*, New York: Hyperion, p. xiv.

species. It confers upon us a considerable evolutionary advantage yet also creates our vulnerability to emotional suffering.

The evolutionary advantage of automatic pilot

As mentioned previously, the restricted capacity of our conscious attention allows us to only attend to a limited amount of information in any given moment. This might give the impression that our conscious attention would restrict us, but the effect of our ability to engage in activity while on automatic pilot enables us to go beyond its limits. The first phase of learning a new skill demands all the limited attention that we have available. Gradually, as we acquire the skill the task becomes automatic to us. We can simultaneously take the conscious attention elsewhere while continuing to engage in the task.

> The brain is a learning system. As neurons connect together into assemblies and assemblies into patterns, the brain is changing: new neurons are forming, and new connections between them are being made. Gradually the threshold for the firing of a whole pattern is lowered. We have learned a task.
> (Williams, 2008)

The fact that we do not have to engage conscious attention on the various elements of familiar activities enables us to simultaneously carry out a range of exceedingly complex tasks. The ability to carry out practical physical activities such as driving, walking or typing, while part of our processing is on automatic pilot, is an important and adaptive skill. The harmful effects of automatic pilot arise when it is carried over to the ways in which we process our emotional experience.

The vulnerability created by automatic pilot

Linked to our ability to learn complex tasks, we have highly developed problem-solving skills. We can reflect, analyse, move our thought processes into the past and future, learn from past experience and apply this learning to future advantage and we can monitor discrepancies between desired outcomes and the status quo. These cognitive "doing mode" skills are crucial foundations to managing many of the challenges of our lives.

In the same ways that our skills with practical activities become part of our automatic repertoire, so this style of habitual problem-solving thinking also becomes automatised. Often beyond our conscious awareness our thinking mind is engaged in judging, monitoring, and problem solving aspects of our internal and external experiences. These analytic problem-solving skills, which bring benefit in so many areas of our lives, can actually increase our difficulties when they are brought to bear on our experience of emotional challenge.

Much of the activity of the ruminative doing mode of mind is happening out of our awareness, and the effects on our emotional experiencing can be catastrophic. It is almost as if we had climbed onto a train at one station and we are carried many, many miles away without realising what is happening. At a certain point, we "come to" and our awareness of the present moment re-establishes itself. As we climb out of the train, the (emotional) landscape that we find ourselves in can be significantly different. So, it is that through a style of processing experience, which is so habitual that it can take place automatically, moods can spiral downwards without the person realising until it is too late—depression has reasserted itself.

In relation to the connection between potential depressive relapse and automatic pilot, there are a number of processes in action which increase the likelihood of a downward spiral being triggered:

1   The mind is operating in habitual ways, which are likely to involve ruminative and avoidant styles of processing, so the person cannot make conscious choices about how to respond to internal or external experiences.

2   The activities of the mind will be having an effect on the emotional experience of the person without them being immediately aware of this.
3   The person has a narrowed, constricted awareness of the present moment and so cannot perceive the range of choices available.

Mindful awareness and automatic pilot

The state of being intentionally, mindfully aware of present-moment experience is completely opposite to the state of automatic pilot:

- Rather than the mind being "caught" by whatever presents itself, there is a conscious intention to direct the attention to a chosen object.
- Rather than the attention being primarily engaged on concepts it is engaged on the direct felt sensory experience of the physicality of the moment.
- Rather than analysing and making judgements about experience the pervading attitude is one of openness and acceptance.

Crucially, training in mindfulness does not involve trying to get rid of problematic patterns of mind—this would only serve to strengthen them. As will be discussed in the next Point, the problematic automatic patterns of mind that are the target of MBCT arise in and are perpetuated by the doing mode of mind. It becomes clear, then, that they cannot be effectively addressed by this same mind mode, as any strategy arising from here will only serve to further proliferate more of this "doing" style of processing. MBCT therefore offers participants a training in accessing and dwelling in the "being mode" of mind, in which the intention is to learn ways of being more fully within the actuality of present-moment experience alongside learning to relate to it with acceptance and friendliness.

Summary

Automatic pilot involves being "out of touch" with direct experience arising in the moment. The effect of being persistently "out of touch" in this way is a disconnection from actual reality and a consequent creation and proliferation of internally created reality. For those with a history of depression this creates the conditions in which a doing mode, ruminative, avoidant style of processing can take hold beyond conscious awareness.

5

Modes of mind: "doing"

An essential premise of MBCT is that the mind has two broad modes through which experience can be processed—doing mode and being mode. A key skill being learnt through MBCT is to recognise which mode of mind one is operating within, and to gain skills in consciously disengaging from one mode of mind and entering another when it is skilful to do so. The problems potentially created through dwelling persistently in a doing mode of mind are particularly highlighted during depression but are familiar to everyone.

Characteristics of doing mode

"Doing mode" is entered when the mind registers discrepancies between an *idea* of how things are and an *idea* of how we want them to be or how we do not want them to be (Segal et al., 2002). Essentially, doing mode relates to the goal-orientated strategies we engage in to:

• reduce the gap between a desired state and how we are experiencing things now (moving towards what we want);

or to:

• keep the gap open between an undesired state and how we are experiencing things now (moving away from what we do not want).

27

This striving towards what we want and away from what we do not want creates, and is driven by, a perpetual and all-pervading sense of dissatisfaction with the way things are.

Doing mode is primarily a conceptual, thought-based mode of processing experience: we are "thinking about" rather than "being with" our direct experience. The thoughts that are the "currency" of this mode of mind become our reality and we judge our experience, the world and decide our actions on the assumption that they are true. Attention is placed largely either in the past or in the future. We are out of touch with "felt" internal experiencing and with experiencing of the world. We can be in doing mode while engaged in activity or while being still. Rather than being descriptive of what we are "doing", it describes how we relate to what is arising for us internally and externally.

The "doing mode" style of processing experience is configured in such a way that it remains in action on a particular "problem" until it is resolved. Another problem or task may become a greater priority temporarily, but the mind will go back to the original issue as soon as a space occurs. The mind therefore remains perpetually active via an engagement in strategies, which are intended to either close or maintain the gap between where we want or do not want to be and where we actually are (Williams, Teasdale, Segal, & Kabat-Zinn, 2007b).

These doing mode "discrepancy-based processing" strategies (Segal et al., 2002) are crucial to our wellbeing and survival. The human skill of being able to move our thought processes into the past and future confers on us an important evolutionary advantage—it enables us to reflect, solve problems and analyse; to learn from the past and to apply this learning to future advantage. Our ability to monitor discrepancies enables us to be highly skilled problem solvers. The goal orientation enables us to keep on task and to improve things. These cognitive skills are highly valued in our culture. We become skilled in the arena of thinking and conceptualising, often to the exclusion of other ways of experiencing.

Summary

The key features of doing mode of mind are:

- goal or problem orientation;
- attention is caught up in concepts and thoughts "about" experience rather than being in touch with the direct sensory experience of the moment;
- attention is predominantly focused on thoughts about the past or the future; and
- there is an absence of acceptance—the mind is scrutinising experience against a perceived sense of how things *should* be. The focus is on striving to make things different from how they are now.

When we engage with practical tasks and problems the doing mode style of processing can be highly suitable. However, these well-developed doing-mode strategies, which bring benefit in so many areas of our lives, can actually serve to increase our suffering and difficulties when we bring them to bear on the experience of our emotions. The next two Points describe the key aspects of doing mode that create this damaging way of processing emotions—rumination and experiential avoidance. Later we will see how approaching difficult emotions from an entirely new perspective—through a "being mode" of mind—offers the possibility of discovering a way to step out of negative cycles and to turn towards rather than away from experience.

6

Doing mode in action: the effects of rumination

The course has helped me to be aware of what my mind does . . . this is invaluable to me—previously my thoughts were in the driving seat of my life without me realising it.
(Keith, MBCT course participant)

The theoretical basis for MBCT describes how the interconnected relapse-related processes of ruminative thinking and experiential avoidance (see Point 7) arise out of and are perpetuated by the activities of the doing mode of mind. Rumination is an attempt to address difficult emotions through a process of analysis and problem solving. It is a goal-driven conceptual process of monitoring "what is" in relation to what is desired, required, expected or feared with the intention of solving or eliminating the problem. All the markers of doing mode of mind summarised at the end of Point 5 apply to rumination.

Typically, people who have a ruminative thinking style spend a lot of time conceptualising their experience, trying to find solutions to their emotional "problems" and analysing why they are feeling this way. The content of ruminative thinking processes often tends to relate to self and to be critical of self—"Why do I feel the way I do? Why has this problem arisen? Why do these things always happen to me? Why am I so useless at sorting this?" . . . and so on. While we are relating to ourselves and the world through a ruminative thinking pattern, our "reality" tends to becomes the content of these thoughts and concepts. We thus become separated from the actuality of experience and lose awareness of what is happening in and around us. If our "view" from this state is that we are inadequate and worthless, then these thoughts are seen as an accurate reflection of reality. Aspects of experience—thoughts, emotions and physical sensations—are judged as good or bad. This in itself gives them a more enduring reality and creates an impetus to act to get rid of the bad and hang on to the good. There is a tendency for thinking to be critical and judgemental, repetitive and circular. Analogous to a car spinning in a muddy rut, the ruminative thinking cycle digs us deeper into well-worn, habitual mental grooves or ruts.

Rumination and emotions

Doing mode is sensitively configured to engage with and attempt to change experiences that do not fit with what we want and aspects of the world that we want to change. When the problem is external, for example posting a letter, doing mode reminds us there is a task to be done, gets us to the post box and only switches off the intention when the letter is posted. The consequence is that the world has changed. Doing mode has done its job. However, when the "problem" that is being tackled is the experience of sadness or unhappiness, the consequences are unintended and unfortunate. The effects of the attempt to "solve" sadness or unhappiness through ruminative doing mode create the vulnerability factors that can lead to depression.

Consider for a moment applying these styles of processing to a difficult emotion such as unhappiness. The mind immediately focuses on the mismatches between the desired state (happiness) and the present state (unhappiness). The ruminative wheels move into action. Alongside a concept of what is being experienced now, an image of the "longed for" peace of mind will arise, plus (for those with a history of depression) a memory of the feared consequence of feeling sad. The discrepancy between current experience and this "feared" or "longed for" experience will persistently be monitored to see how progress is being made in the goal to reduce the gap (in relation to getting what is wanted) or to maintain the gap (in relation to avoiding what is not wanted). The image of what is most wanted—peace of mind—alongside the experience of sadness creates a heightened sense of how unsatisfactory things are—this in itself *increases* the sadness. The image of what is most not wanted—depression—creates a heightened sense of the need to redouble attempts to ensure that this feeling does not get worse. Greater effort is placed on solving this problem through the ruminative thinking process, which has the unhappy effect of further perpetuating these loops (Williams et al., 2007b). The irony is that the true problem is not now the original sadness, it is the escalation of feeling upset and hopeless caused by the doing mode ruminative strategies that are triggered at times when we register a challenging emotion.

Summary

Rumination is propelled by an attempt to solve an emotional "problem". Essentially, there is no long-term solution to these difficult experiences—they are an aspect of the constantly fluxing experience of being human. Our emotional life is not a problem to be solved and yet we have a tendency to live as if it was. Attempts to address difficult emotions through a ruminative problem-solving mode of mind are doomed to failure. In itself, sadness is not a problem it is an innate part of being human but if we endeavour to avoid it by trying to "fix", manipulate or struggle with it, a passing sadness can lead to persistent unhappiness.

7

Doing mode in action: the effects of experiential avoidance

Aversive reactions to unwanted emotions such as sadness are the first step in a potential cascade towards a persistent sense of unhappiness or depression. A key result of aversive reacting is experiential avoidance—the attempt to remain out of contact with our thoughts, emotions and body sensations. Hayes, Wilson, Gifford, Follette, and Strosahl (1996) suggested that the attempt to avoid internal experiences is a process that is both common across many psychological problems and implicated in their maintenance; and at the other end of the spectrum high levels of experiential connectedness (of both client and therapist) are positively correlated with good outcomes in therapy. Developing skills to "tune into" the direct experience of what has been avoided through meditation is a distinctive feature of MBCT (Williams et al., 2007b).

The instinct to avoid the unpleasant

A crucial part of our natural survival processes is our aversive reaction to unpleasant feelings. It makes clear sense that we are wired to avoid or escape dangers such as an oncoming car or a charging bull (Williams et al., 2007b). However, the tendency to react in this same avoidant way to internal signals of threat in the form of unwanted emotions, negative thoughts or difficult body sensations does not promote our wellbeing. Instead it acts to add layers of difficulty on top of the original challenge. The attempt to run away from internal experience is futile—in the end we still have to live with ourselves and our experience. The tendency to struggle with, fight and attempt to get rid of unwanted internal experience creates a "battle zone" within the mind: mindfulness teaches a way to help us step aside from this struggle.

The habitual pattern of avoiding the experience of unwanted emotions is a pervasive human tendency familiar to all at some level. For those with a history of experiencing persistent painful emotions and moods, the wish to escape or avoid internal experience is understandable. However, not only does this create the desired disconnection from or suppression of difficult experience, it also creates a general disconnection—a sense of being damped down, narrowed and constricted. It reduces the capacity to respond wisely to difficult experience. It also, as shall be seen in Point 8, shuts down adaptive approach-related behaviours such as kindliness, interest, presence and warmth.

Although the broad spectrum of experience—pleasant, unpleasant and neutral—is explored within the sessions, there is a bias in MBCT towards developing skills in noticing our habitually avoidant reactions to unpleasant experiences. As discussed previously, these are particularly implicated in the chain of reactions that can increase vulnerability to depressive relapse.

Rumination and avoidance

Rumination is intricately entwined with experiential avoidance—they are both strategies that are motivated by the attempt to get away from difficult emotional experience. On the face of it, rumination seems to keep one engaged with the problem in hand, so how does it act to ensure that experience is avoided? One possible way in which experiential avoidance and rumination are linked is that both arise out of our fear of feeling the intense sensations associated with our emotions. It can become habitual to deal with emotions by switching into a conceptual brooding problem-solving mode (rumination). In doing this we are erecting a "smokescreen" through which we suppress or disconnect from difficult emotions (experiential avoidance).

Avoidance fuelling the creation of layers of suffering

Gunaratana succinctly said, "pain is inevitable, suffering is not" (2002, p. 99). He was pointing towards the premise, central to Buddhist philosophy, that there is a distinction between the basic pain of feelings (which is inevitable) and the immediate contraction of mind and body to avoid this pain (which is not inevitable). Welwood (2000) talked of the layers of suffering that we habitually add to primary difficulty—the long-term, stress-related consequences of propping up an identity that is based on avoidance and denial. Essentially acceptance is emphasised so strongly in the MBCT programme because its opposite—avoidance—is so risky (Segal et al., 2002). Mindfulness practice is a training process that enables us to clearly see these habitual avoidant patterns. Through this we can learn to reduce the "extra" that we add to the basic pain of feelings. An essential premise of MBCT, therefore, is that pain is *an* aspect of the overall "tapestry" of our life and that it is the avoidance of this reality that creates emotional difficulty.

Summary

Rumination and the avoidance of direct experience while on automatic pilot are interconnected vulnerability factors for triggering depressive relapse. The particular effects of this mix are:

1   The *ruminative thinking process* labels unwanted emotions as "problems", endeavouring to get rid of them. Its lack of success in this endeavour triggers and maintains a downward spiral.
2   *Experiential avoidance* of difficult material adds further layers of struggle and tension and creates reservoirs of unprocessed material.

3   Because the mind is engaged on thinking plus there is an urge to avoid experience, awareness of present-moment sensory experiencing is fragmented or absent—*processing of experience is happening on autopilot.* Experiencing becomes "narrowed" and our view constricted. In this state it becomes unlikely that the small beauties and pleasures of life are seen or appreciated, further compounding the challenges being experienced.

8

Reacting and responding to experience: avoidance and approach

Habitual patterns of experiential avoidance are one of the key planks that trigger and maintain depression. A distinctive feature therefore of MBCT is its emphasis on learning how to notice and then intentionally transform these patterns through choosing to turn towards or "approach" experience.

Approach and avoidance mode

The human brain has two mutually inhibitive configurations, which are triggered by our innate survival instincts but which are also amenable to shaping through training the mind (Davidson, Kabat-Zinn, & Schumacher, 2003). One of these configurations is a *mode of avoidance*, which is triggered by threats and a need to take self-preserving action such as physical avoidance or defensive attack. It involves the fight/flight reaction, in which the whole system is engaged in fighting or in running from a perceived threat. Avoidance mode can be triggered by situations requiring a physical response (such as leaping out of the way of an oncoming car). It can also be triggered by situations for which a physical response is not appropriate, but which are nevertheless perceived as threatening (such as waking up in the morning with a sense of hopelessness). Avoidance is associated with an increase in activation of the right frontal lobe of the brain relative to the left. The other configuration is a *mode of approach* in which there is a movement towards experience and a sense of welcome and openness to it. Approach is associated with an increase in activation on the left frontal lobe relative to the right. Note the key difference between the approach stance and attachment. Approach has the potential to be even handed towards all our experience while attachment is marked by disappointment and frustration when "positive" things end.

Richard Davidson's work[3] in investigating the patterns of activity of the brain when operating in approach or avoidance mode has clearly demonstrated that training in mindfulness leads to an increase in activity in the left frontal lobe of the brain (the area associated with approach) even when participants were undergoing an experimentally induced negative mood. Mindfulness skills thus enable the person to approach their experience—pleasant or unpleasant—with a sense of openness and willingness to experience it as it is. The effect of being in approach mode to experience is that we have greater opportunity to respond consciously, rather than react unconsciously, to internal and external events. The essential premise here is that we are less at the mercy of our moods if we are open to experiencing the natural changes and flux of sensation in the body, thoughts and emotions.

Developing the ability to be in "approach" mode towards experience

How does training in mindfulness support us to learn to operate more from approach mode? The body is constantly engaged in a process of receiving sensory impressions. They are immediately registered as a "feeling tone" of pleasant, unpleasant or neutral. The mind-body system on a biological level instinctively reacts to these through either "approach" or "avoidance" mode. This

---

3 Davidson et al., 2003, researched the effects of offering an eight-week Mindfulness-Based Stress Reduction programme to a group of employees in a biotech company. Brain scanning images of the group who had taken the eight-week programme demonstrated an increase in relative activity in the left frontal lobe of the brain in comparison with their colleagues in the control group.

occurs beyond conscious awareness, but from this point on we have the capacity to learn to bring attention and acceptance to the sensations in the body that mark these movements into "approach" or "avoidance". Awareness of these sensory experiences enables us to "tune into" the signal that an avoidant pattern has been activated. Often the simple act of bringing kindly attention to sensations such as restlessness, tightness or constriction interrupts a habitual downward chain of challenging thoughts, body sensations, emotions and behaviour. In that micro-moment we have moved from avoidance into approach mode.

This process can be seen as a retraining in how sensory information is recognised and subsequently processed. Through formal and informal mindfulness practices we are learning to become aware of the physical sensations that are arising in connection with the perception of pleasant and unpleasant experience; to identify precise places in the body where these are arising and to acknowledge emotions and thoughts that arise in connection with these sensations. Through all this we are learning to see the layers that are habitually added to the perception of experience; we recognise the particular "lens" through which we see the world. This lens is created by the mental processes that are constantly assimilating current perception of experience with that of accumulated previous experience.

Learning to respond rather than react

The overriding emphasis throughout a mindfulness-based course is on developing the possibility of responding skilfully by seeing clearly the tendency we all have to react habitually. When we are experiencing challenging emotions it is understandable that we react to try and get rid of or avoid them. The basis of the MBCT programme is that these habitual reactions are part of the pattern that maintains and worsens difficult emotions. Rather than putting our energies into avoiding our experience (with the struggle and tension that this involves), we are learning to pause and be with our experience as it is. Present-moment acceptance thus becomes a foundation from which we have the choice to respond in wiser ways.

Summary

The processes of avoidance, approach and subsequent reaction or response that have been described in this Point can be summarised thus:

- MBCT participants are learning to directly perceive sensory experience in the body. This facilitates the earlier perception of signals of aversion: reactive patterns to unpleasant experience that become part of an experientially avoidant style of processing. If we stay in automatic pilot as these avoidant patterns are activated, there is the risk of moving into an unhelpful style of processing.
- Bringing mindful awareness (with its orientation of kindly interest) to the activation of these avoidant patterns, in and of itself, changes the processing to an approach style.
- From this position of wider awareness of "in-the-moment" sensory experiencing plus an orientation of "approach" towards experience, we are better able to respond wisely.

The central premise of MBCT, therefore, is that the first step in relating differently involves an accepting and allowing of things as they are. Ultimately, acceptance enables us to see more clearly what, if anything, needs to change.

9

Modes of mind: "being"

> *Imagine a life in which what is actually happening in the*
> *moment is what really counts . . . Calmness and alertness*
> *exist together. You are truly alive and awake.*
>
> (Melissa Blacker[4])

As described in Point 5, a central premise of MBCT is that the mind operates in different modes. A key intention of the programme is to enable participants to recognise the mode of mind that they are in, and to be able to intentionally shift from one mode to another. This happens in the moment—the ability to "wake up" while in the midst of things in daily life can take the form of a momentary sense of awareness of the sensations of the feet on the floor or of the breath. In that moment, instead of being caught up with whatever mind state predominates we change perspective; we can be aware of what is happening; an opportunity has opened up to think and act differently.

As discussed previously, working with difficult emotions through the medium of doing mode takes us towards suffering. Tackling a building project might best be accomplished through engaging our faculties of doing. It is of course possible to infuse our "doing" with qualities of "being", which facilitates us in staying present with the moment-by-moment process of moving towards a future goal and in bringing qualities of acceptance and moderation to the striving towards it. An implicit

4 From "Meditation" by Melissa Blacker in M. A. Bright (ed.), *Holistic Health and Healing*, Philadelphia: F. A. Davis Company, p. 105.

understanding of MBCT is that in order to live a balanced and healthy life we need to cultivate and know both doing and being modes, so that we can be flexible and responsive to what is most needed in each moment.

Given that the majority of people (particularly in Western cultures) are trained to operate predominantly in doing mode, and that the problematic patterns of mind, which are the target of MBCT, arise and proliferate within doing mode, the overriding emphasis in the programme is to facilitate participants in experiencing being mode. An important way in which this is conveyed is through the teacher embodying the qualities of "being" during the teaching (see Point 30).

So, what is the experience of being? It has to be experienced to be fully understood and so the teaching methods used in MBCT are predominantly experiential, which enables participants to be guided towards tasting an experience of "being". Participants are then supported in exploring this direct experience and opening to new learning that can be put to use in working with difficulties in everyday life. Accepting the inadequacy of language, the following describes the key characteristics of "being mode" of mind:

- attention is *intentionally* placed on present-moment experiencing;
- the person is in touch with the world directly through their senses—seeing, hearing, smelling, feeling and tasting;
- experience is held within an attitudinal framework characterised by acceptance, kindliness, interest, warmth and non-striving; and
- all experience is perceived as events within the field of awareness.

The felt experience of dwelling in being mode is one of connectedness with internal experience and with the world around us, of vibrancy, of immediacy, and of a sense of the multidimensional complexity and interconnectedness of self, life and the world. Whether the experience of the moment is pleasant or unpleasant there is an intimacy with all that is encountered.

Developing this greater connection with experience is a mixture of pleasure and pain. Sally's experience of taking the course typified this. She came because of a long struggle with repeated bouts of depression, initially triggered after the birth of each of her two daughters but now occurring without apparent reason. Her developing awareness helped her to spontaneously connect with her life in a way that was new to her; whereas previously her days had been filled with tasks to be done, she now found herself enjoying the moments of walking to school with her children; she rediscovered her old delight in the plants emerging in her garden in the spring. She also found herself intensely feeling for the first time the rawness of the pain of her mother's death, which had happened some years before. Underneath each of the pleasures she was experiencing was a deep sadness that her mother was not with her to appreciate all this—to see her grandchildren growing up so beautifully; to see the clematis that she had given her come back into flower again. At times over the weeks of the course she felt overcome with emotion and waves of sobbing would move through her. In this way though she was gradually opening to "what is", and gently putting herself back in connection with aspects of her experience that had been cut off. This can be an inherently painful process and yet for Sally was accompanied by a tremendous sense of relief that she could now properly grieve. The teaching process within the MBCT programme is intended to offer a contained space within which this difficult work can take place.

Cultivating being mode

The means towards experiencing and cultivating "being mode" is the development of awareness and acceptance through the practice of mindfulness meditation. There are two aspects to this process—known sometimes as calming or "concentration"[5] practices and "insight" practices. Both are woven into the teaching throughout, but there is a greater emphasis on learning to calm, settle and gather the mind in the first half of the programme.

Once having settled into a posture for the mindfulness practice, the first step is to intentionally take the focus of attention to a specific, tangible experience within the body—the movement of breath in a particular place is a common focus of attention. This deliberate cultivation of detailed attention in a specific place has the effect of facilitating a disengagement from analytic (doing mode of mind) thought processes. This occurs partly because the focus on the breath takes up attentional capacity that would normally be used to ruminate, but also the direct perception of physical sensations in the body allows us to gradually become more aware of a different realm of experience. Most periods of formal practice start with this narrow angle focus of attention, to facilitate gathering and settling the mind.

The second aspect is to bring an intention of investigation into what arises as we simultaneously hold the intention to be attentive to sensations of breath. In gathering the attention in this way we are coming into relationship with our own mind. We are creating an opening in which it becomes possible to discern patterns in the mind: the ways the mind moves into automatic habits, the attitudes that arise and the ways in which layers are added to the direct experience in the moment. We are gradually coming to know the mind as it is.

Of course, as we practice in this way all the tendencies, habits and struggles that manifest themselves in our daily life will be presented to us! The likelihood is that doing mode will

---

5 The word concentration is used here to indicate gathering the attention and bringing it together in one place rather than an effortful act of concentration. Sometimes concentration practices are known as "settling" practices.

assert itself again and again—we can just as easily make a "project" out of bringing the attention back to the breath as we can out of anything else in life. Essentially, the invitation is to come to see each time the mind slips away from the chosen object of attention (e.g. the breath) and to bring it back. We are not *trying* to keep the mind on the breath—we are learning to wake up more often to the times when the mind wanders off into automatic habitual patterns and to recognise these tendencies for what they are.

One can liken this process to training the body when we exercise. In the process of bringing the mind back again and again to a chosen object we are training the "muscle" of attention. As we persist in practicing in this way, we are gradually more able to access a greater continuity of awareness—an experience of "being with" the arising of experience. Awareness is always there in each moment. It is simply obscured from view by the activities of our mind, with all its analysing, judging, comparing, remembering, anticipating and planning. Each of these is critically important for managing many of life's tasks, but they tend to dominate the mind even when they are unnecessary and unhelpful.

Summary

Participants are learning to use their developing skills in working with their attention to cultivate the potential to change "mental gears" in each moment. They are learning to discern when and how to shift from doing mode into being mode. Much of the MBCT programme is dedicated to training participants in a methodology—mindfulness meditation—which offers a means to access being mode of mind.

.

10

Body sensations—a door into the present

To come to our senses, both literally and metaphorically, on the big scale as a species and on the smaller scale as a single human being, we first need to return to the body, the locus within which the biological senses and what we call the mind arise.

(Jon Kabat-Zinn[6])

Training in mindfulness places a great deal of emphasis on learning to be with direct experience as it arises in the body. With the teacher's support participants are engaged during the practices and the dialogue that follows in identifying precise places within the body where sensations are arising and in describing the sensations themselves. This is the starting place for understanding the nature of direct experiencing and for learning to re-inhabit the body. The body is the most accessible ground of our direct experience in the present moment (Welwood, 2000).

All our thoughts, emotions, speech and action are (whether we are *aware* of it or not) guided by background felt meanings, which are expressed through our experiencing in our body. Taking the space to pause, be with and allow an intuitive knowing of our experience to emerge offers a different way to approach the challenges of our lives. We had this ability to "know" through our body before we were able to talk. The price we pay for being a language-based species is that labelling

6 Kabat-Zinn, 2005, *Coming To Our Senses*, New York: Hyperion, p. 10.

our experience offers us a means to objectify and separate from it. In our predominantly verbal way of feeling and expressing ourselves it can feel counterintuitive to move into the body and allow the body to reveal to us what is here. One of the processes taking place in a mindfulness-based course is learning to trust in this unfolding and to allow space for this more intuitive, intimate knowing and understanding to emerge. Ultimately, the learning and insight that arises in this visceral way may be integrated with our thinking processes and even articulated verbally—the dialogue that happens within a mindfulness-based course facilitates a "translation" of felt sense into integrated learning—but initially it starts with patiently experiencing the flux of things within the body.

Coming to "feel" our experience involves re-learning the ability to directly perceive through our senses of hearing, smelling, seeing, tasting, touching and the kinaesthetic sense of just feeling sensations in our body. This level of awareness and discernment of direct experience allows us to take a more accurate moment-by-moment "read out" of the "barometer" of the body—using the body as an indicator of how we are experiencing things.

Learning to re-inhabit the body

Reversing the habitual tendency to retreat from experience in the body is a challenging and painful process. Denise, like many with a history of depression, had come to feel safer thinking "about" her emotions rather than experiencing them in her body. The work that she and fellow participants were engaged in on the MBCT programme made rational sense to her—she knew that there was a lot of her life that she kept "at bay" and that this was part of what was perpetuating her depression. The reality of working with this became a painful and long process of bit-by-bit "reclaiming" parts of her experience that had been pushed away. It started with the body scan when just the seemingly simple process of lying on the floor and taking her attention through her body connected her to physical pain that she did not know she had. She discovered that her body was habitually gripped with tightness. The process of softening and opening physically began to allow Denise to experience old sadness. She began to see how ingrained her habit of discounting these experiences over the years was. It was not easy and, like many, she struggled with learning to access her bodily sensations. It is a process that takes time and gentle persistence. The support from her teacher within the sessions helped her to stay with this process and to work as best she could with it. Denise's experience of participation in an MBCT programme was very different from what might have happened in other forms of psychotherapy. In MBCT she was being encouraged to see how her experience was arising moment by moment rather than dwelling in the story of how these sad happenings had occurred in her life.

Although understandable, the effect of avoidance and disconnection is, first, that the processing of emotional experience remains incomplete and, second, the continuing effort needed to keep unwanted emotions at bay creates additional layers of tension, stress and tightness in the body. The body can be seen as a "window onto the mind": it is through the body that the healing process of completing the unfinished work of emotional processing can take place (Segal et al., 2002). Being present with experience in the body is very different from any attempt to "understand" or "analyse" emotions or their origins.

Another way to be with thoughts and emotions

It quickly becomes clear to mindfulness-based course participants, as the practice unfolds, that their thoughts are intimately connected with their body sensations and that emotions are in essence a constellation of fluxing sensations, thoughts and feelings in the body. While the intention throughout the practice is to learn to be less identified with experience—to see thoughts, emotions and sensations as events in the field of awareness—this tends to come more easily with some aspects of our experience than with others. Our thoughts and emotions tend to have a personal quality to them, which makes them *feel* like aspects of "me". The invitation to explore a new way of being with thoughts and emotions through shifting attention into the body and experiencing where and how they are manifesting physically can be tremendously helpful. In residing with tangible sensations as they unfold in each moment, there is less opportunity to be carried away into the story about me and my experience. The body can reveal some interesting information about how this experience, registered initially by a thought stream or an emotion, is being felt and processed.

Using the body as an ally

As discussed in Point 2, the body is part of the feedback loop that maintains depression. The sensations of heaviness, fatigue, sagging posture and muscle tightness associated with the experience of depression can be one of the factors perpetuating the experience. Seeing this offers some important clues in learning to use the body as an ally in reversing the direction of the feedback loops. This can be as simple as attending to our posture while engaged in a mindfulness practice. In adopting an upright, dignified position, which is stable and grounded and simultaneously relaxed and open, we are embodying the qualities that we intend to cultivate and sending a powerful message to our mind—we are conveying to ourselves an attitudinal stance of relaxed attentiveness, readiness, willingness and availability.

Summary

Directly experiencing sensations within the body provides another place from which to view and be with experience and a different vantage point for relating to thoughts. Mindfulness practice offers a direct, intuitive way of knowing experience.

11

Ways of approaching and welcoming what is

> *This being human is a guest house.*
> *Every morning a new arrival.*
> *A joy, a depression, a meanness,*
> *some momentary awareness comes*
> *as an unexpected visitor.*
> *Welcome and entertain them all!*
> (Rumi[7])

Investigating the possibility of reversing the instinctive trend to retreat from difficulty and to actually "lay out a red carpet" for our unwanted feelings is a core theme of the MBCT programme, especially in the second half. By the time participants are presented explicitly with this possibility midway through the programme, they will have had several weeks of practicing "being with what is": of working to gently cultivate acceptance of unhelpful habits of mind within their daily mindfulness practice. Plenty of unwanted experience will have spontaneously emerged in this time. *The Guest House* poem by Rumi (see above), which is shared with participants, points to how this is taken a step further, by cultivating a deliberate, intentional "turning towards" and "inviting in" of our difficulties. This is a further step along the road of training the mind to operate more and more in "approach" mode in relation to experience. This Point explores acceptance and being with difficulty in the MBCT programme in terms of:

7 Barks et al. (translators), 1995, "The Guest House" from *The Essential Rumi*, San Francisco: Harper, p. 109.

- the "flavour" and spirit of acceptance;
- the layers within acceptance;
- the underpinning learning that supports acceptance; and
- the paradoxes inherent in the process.

The flavour and spirit of acceptance

Acceptance can be confused with resignation and giving up. It certainly involves giving up the struggle against our experience, so it can be contrasted with resistance. It engages us in a turning toward (opening to) rather than a turning away (closing down) from present-moment experience. Within this we are learning to be present with and acceptant of pleasant, unpleasant and neutral experience—developing an even-handedness towards our experience. There is an aim to cultivate a willingness to let things be as they are as we become aware of them whether we like them or not; then we include the "liking" and the "not liking" as simply an aspect of our whole experience.

The spirit we bring to the process of acceptance is important. It has an open quality, which is part of the attitudinal stance of willingness to be available to our experience. We learn to be tender, gentle, kindly, compassionate and respectful towards ourselves and our experience.

The layers within acceptance

Acceptance does not require us to immediately and unreservedly open the doors to difficult experience. If it feels overwhelming we may simply "take a peek at it", and at best we can bring acceptance to the struggle that arises as we consider the possibility of letting our experience be as it is. Within all of this there is understanding and compassion towards ourselves of how hard this work is: how hot and painful our difficulties are and how sensitive and gentle we need to be towards ourselves when we are experiencing difficulty and vulnerability.

During the dialogue in week 5 of the MBCT programme, Doug vividly described an experience of moving towards difficulty, which occurred during the sitting practice at the beginning of the session. Within this practice, the teacher had invited participants to bring to mind a current difficulty and to come to a sense of how this experience might be expressing itself within the body. Doug's difficult situation related to a disagreement that he had had with his boss the previous week. Since then he had been churning this situation over and over in his mind, and he was feeling stuck with his anger and guilt. This was the first time that he had taken the opportunity to turn towards the "feeling" of it. He described the locus of this experience as being a contracted and "knotted" area in the centre of his body. Initially, he spent time "viewing" this while keeping his attention connected with sensations in his breath, aware of an increase in his heart rate that was connected to the thought of what it might be like to open to these sensations. After some time, as he described it, he "dipped his toe in the water": guiding his attention towards this area using the breath as he had learnt to do while practising the body scan, he lingered with awareness around the edges of the knot exploring the sensations that were within and around it. In doing this he discovered that within this overall sense of "knot" and contraction there was an interesting collection of "tendrils" of fluxing sensation. In that moment his relationship with this experience had changed from one of fear and avoidance to one of curiosity and approach.

Doug later described how his whole orientation to this difficulty shifted—he felt less angry with himself, he felt more understanding of his boss and he felt less preoccupied by the incident. Over the weeks, Doug began experimenting further with this way of working with difficult experience, discovering that he could play with it in a number of ways depending on the intensity of the experience and how he was feeling in that moment. He found that he could move and "be within" the experience: feeling, exploring and investigating the web of sensations at the heart of it. At other times he used the possibility of moving to and fro between the difficult experience and present awareness of the breath in the body. Throughout this process he, like other participants, was working up to and exploring the "edge" of what is possible in each moment.

The experience for many of us is that our protective defences are well constructed and will move firmly into place when things feel overwhelming. In exploring this new possibility of moving up towards difficult experience, we have not lost our well-rehearsed and often appropriate strategies to step back from intensity. This can gradually instil a confidence that with gentle persistence we can keep working to bring attention to difficulty at a pace that is right for each of us. Gradually, the defensive strategies that keep things at bay are less needed and dissolve of their own accord, in their own time, without force.

The underpinning learning that supports acceptance

The first half of the MBCT programme offers participants training in underpinning skills. This serves them in good stead when there is an explicit invitation to explore and invite difficulty into awareness. They will therefore already be in process with learning to:

- use awareness of specific sensations in the body as an anchor into the present moment to support them in *responding* from a place of connection to sensations rather than *reacting* from a disconnected thought "about" how things actually are;
- recognise and "let be" judgements and automatic patterns;
- develop a sense of compassion and friendly curiosity about the detail of experience (which changes avoidance mode into approach mode);
- see clearly the "extra" suffering that avoidance causes; and

- develop a new attitudinal stance of allowing, rather than perpetually striving to make things different from how they actually are.

Significantly, the spirit of welcoming and turning towards is being conveyed to the participants throughout by the teacher embodying these qualities during the teaching. This becomes part of the teacher's approach to each aspect of the teaching process—preparing for the sessions, greeting participants as they arrive and relating with them and all that arises during the class.

Paradoxes inherent in the process

Paradoxically, acceptance of the present can be a place from which change arises. Mindfulness-based participants engage with the programme in the hope of arriving at different states, yet through the repeated exposure to mindfulness practice and process they are being taught to simply experience what is present, moment by moment. They are learning that it might be possible to learn to be at ease with not feeling at ease! Embodying and holding this paradox skilfully, in ways that facilitate participants in engaging fully in the programme and the home practice while simultaneously letting go of the outcome, is a key challenge for teacher and participants alike.

What is going on in the process of acceptance that promotes the possibility of change? In order to come to an acceptance of what is present within us we find that we have let go of the struggle to try to change "what is". Acceptance of the present moment enables us to step aside from the struggle. The additional layers of stress, resistance and tension gradually drop away—the problem becomes less complicated because the "extra" we have added is no longer obscuring the reality underneath. There is a far greater level of awareness of the dimensions of the problem—the subtlety and interconnecting complexity of sensations, emotions and thoughts arising in relation to it. We are therefore better informed about how to responsively manage it. We are likely to be feeling more kindly around this problem and so our response may be flavoured with an intention to be respectful and do no harm to ourselves or others. We are in approach rather than avoidance mode. All in all, the intricate process of being more fully where we actually are in this moment offers a clearer space from which to skilfully respond and make decisions. Change naturally emerges through this.

Inevitably as we discover that acceptance can bring about change, we can find ourselves wanting to use such acceptance as a tool "to fix" ourselves. However, as soon as we invest in wanting things to be other than how they are right now, we find we have moved out of the present; we are back to struggling with our experience. Accepting ourselves as we see the continual arising of the wanting for things to be different is another layer to this process.

Summary

A distinctive feature of MBCT is that it is underpinned by the understanding that "if we cope with our unpleasant feelings by pushing them away or trying to control them, we actually end up maintaining them" (Segal et al., 2002, p. 292). Mindfulness is cultivated as a way of discovering how to do the opposite of this: to be fully with and befriend with warmth and compassion all of our experience—pleasant, unpleasant and neutral. This will not always be a smooth ride. Emotional reactivity and the full range of emotional states available to human beings are as much valid domains of meditative experience as experiences of calm and relaxation. Through this process of learning we come to see that the best way to achieve our goals is often to back off from striving for results and to start seeing and accepting things are they are in the present.

12

Developing a new relationship with experience

> *The endless battle of judgmental voices in my head had caused me so much pain that I'd go to great lengths to suppress them. I began to learn that, however many thought buses came past . . . , I didn't have to catch any of them. I began to let the buses go by, just watching them. This was the single most important thing I learnt in this bout of depression. It seems like nothing, but its effects were huge.*
>
> (Gwyneth Lewis[8])

When interviewed a year after completing an MBCT course, Daniel described that he had suffered a further episode of depression since taking the programme. However, this depression had felt different—he had been able to see it in a wider perspective: as part of the tapestry of his life; as being his experience in this moment; and he had been able to work differently with the experience of being depressed. The episode had not lasted as long. Difficult experiences will continue to be a part of our lives—for some this may include periodic bouts of depression. The possibility, though, of learning to be in a different relationship to these times opens the potential for the experience to feel profoundly different.

As described in Point 2, Segal, Williams, and Teasdale first alighted on mindfulness training as a means to address the

---

8 Lewis, 2002, *Sunbathing in the Rain—A Cheerful Book on Depression*, London: Flamingo, p. 88.

vulnerability to relapse carried by people who are prone to depression because it is a tried and tested methodology for facilitating a "de-centred" or "stepped back" relationship to thoughts. Their analysis of the "depression preventing skills" gained by people who have had CBT during an episode of depression was that they had developed a fundamentally different relationship with their thoughts. They were no longer completely inside their thoughts—they had the ability to see them in perspective and to take a wider view of them. This skill, which develops implicitly through CBT in relation to thoughts, is targeted explicitly in MBCT in connection with all aspects of experience.

The direct experience within mindfulness practice for many participants of perceiving their thoughts in this radically new way is often fleeting and momentary. However, the insight it creates is profound:

> It is remarkable how liberating it feels to be able to see that your thoughts are just thoughts and that they are not "you" or "reality" . . . the simple act of recognizing your thoughts as thoughts can free you from the distorted reality they often create and allow for more clear-sightedness and a greater sense of manageability in your life.
>
> (Kabat-Zinn, 1990, pp. 69–70).

The effects of relating from inside our experience

William James[9], writing in 1870, described the illusion of thought ownership: "each pulse of consciousness, each thought, dies away and is replaced by another . . .". This seemingly endless stream of thinking creates the illusion of a central thinker lying above or behind the mind stream (Welwood,

9 Taken from *The Principles of Psychology* (2007 edn) by William James.

2000). The paradox is that although thoughts arise within us and they are an intimate part of our experience in each moment, they are not us. They do not have an enduring reality that can be pointed to as "me" or "mine". The tendency to relate to our experience in general and our thoughts in particular as representations of reality or fact is the cause of much of our distress and difficulty.

Our thoughts are often driving and controlling us. We are caught inside them. While the ruminative thinking habit that is a key component of the process of depressive relapse is a strong example of this tendency, we can all recognise these processes at play within our own minds. A thought moves into our mind and the body may jump into action without any conscious awareness being engaged. Thoughts swirl in the mind around a particular preoccupation of the moment. They have a compelling feel to them, they demand attention and they colour our existence until they are resolved or another more pressing thought takes over. They simultaneously colour and obscure awareness of the present moment. This is doing mode in action; it is not a mistake that needs remediation—it is what the doing mode of mind is designed for.

Learning to relate to rather than from our experience

At the heart of mindfulness practice is a paradox: it encourages full engagement with our lives while simultaneously stepping back and observing what is going on. This is done with a posture of kindly benevolent curiosity and non-judgemental interest. In particular, negative experiencing is not pushed away or made into our "enemy", but rather we befriend our experience by "acknowledging and letting be" and "turning towards and directly experiencing". In this way we develop a different relationship with our experience—simultaneously participating and observing what arises moment by moment.

The process through which participants begin to learn to relate to thoughts as events in the mind during the formal mindfulness practices falls into two stages. Initially, the invitation is to designate another focus of attention such as the breath to anchor the attention into the present moment. We note the thoughts as they arise, and then let go of them, returning to the primary focus of attention on the breath. This is done with a sense of kindliness and gentleness but also with persistence and firmness. Participants spend a lot of time practicing this—and it is hard. Thoughts can be tenacious and compelling but: "the message is implicit: This is just a thought. In this way participants [are] learning to step back, to de-centre from the content and just notice the thoughts" (Segal et al., 2002, p. 249).

The next step in the learning process is to seek to make thoughts the explicit focus of attention. The encouragement here is to see thoughts in the same way as any other passing event in our mind. The section within the sitting meditation in which "awareness of thoughts as thoughts" is introduced is generally preceded by "awareness of sounds"—this can often help to convey what is intended here. Generally participants are able to taste an experience of a relaxed awareness of sounds arising and passing in the space around them: sounds come and go without us being involved in influencing them. Sounds do not have the personal quality that our thoughts have to us. The invitation is to explore relating to thoughts in just this way—as events passing through the space of the mind. This is a challenging practice but many participants begin to sense the possibility that this is pointing towards. This in itself facilitates a shift towards realising that our thoughts are simply thoughts—they are not facts.

Through persistent practice in these ways participants can become more familiar with the "terrain" of their thoughts and emotions and the process of thinking and feeling. They can discern, through feeling the "flavour" of their thoughts, the mode of mind they are in. They can see more easily what to let be and what to respond to.

Learning that we are more than our experiencing

An implicit message within all this is that we are more than the content of our thoughts, our past experiences, our body sensations, our emotions and so on. All these things are not who we are. It is tremendously freeing and liberating to have this perspective on our experiencing. Participants gradually learn to translate these new ways of relating to experience into their daily lives. They learn to *know* their experiencing as it happens without judging it: "when I'm walking I know that I am walking" or "when I am sad, confused and feel upset, I know that I feel sad, confused and upset and that is how it is right now" (Elias, 2006).

Summary

Mindfulness cultivates skills in both witnessing experience (the "de-centred" aspect of the process) and in engaging and participating directly in the actuality of experience. De-centring involves cultivating the ability not to be identified or lost within experience—for example seeing "thoughts as thoughts" rather than as a representation of reality. Direct engagement with experience involves being with the sensory nature and qualities of it. Participants are learning that we have choices in how we relate to experience.

13

Awareness as a container of our experience

Awareness may not diminish the enormity of our pain in all circumstances. It does provide a greater basket for tenderly holding and intimately knowing our suffering and that is transformative.

(Jon Kabat-Zinn[10])

Awareness (along with the faculty of language) is the feature that distinguishes our species from all others. It leads to tremendous potential for transformation and learning (Kabat-Zinn, 2005). Developing our practice of mindful attention is the way through which we can learn to intentionally access the awareness that is inherently present all the time. MBCT and other mindfulness-based programmes are training us to create the conditions in our lives through which we can clearly see how our awareness is obscured by the unhelpful mind states that habitually dominate our experience.

It can feel tremendously reassuring to hear that awareness can contain any experience that emerges: as Kabat-Zinn says above "tenderly holding it". It is also encouraging to realise that the awareness of our experience is not the experience itself: the awareness of depression is not depressed; the awareness of pain is not itself in pain. This may go part of the way towards explaining why as soon as experience is seen in the light of awareness it has changed in some way. We are no longer inside the experience looking out onto the world through the filter of

10 Kabat-Zinn, 2005, *Coming to Our Senses*, New York: Hyperion, p. 90.

the emotions created by it. We are able to be with this experience, see around it and see it in a wider context. Through seemingly subtle shifts in relationship with experience, radical new perspectives emerge. Kabat-Zinn (2005) talks of how each moment contains the potential for these new perspectives. The process of releasing them and realising them involves "a rotation within the mindscape" (p. 352). We are holding experience in awareness in a particular way, which allows us to see around it: our relationship to it, what we bring to it and what we add to it. In this way our experience is "held" in this wider container of awareness.

In an interview after taking part in an MBCT programme Sharon described her experience of this. Prior to the course she would regularly feel overwhelmed by the intensity of her feelings—her emotions "took on a life of their own". She would try and manage this in the best ways that she could—initially this involved doing lots to distract herself, but the combination of overworking and the lack of sleep that was a feature of these times meant that she would become deeply exhausted. Frequently this was the precursor to depression. The learning that took place during the MBCT programme helped her to be with these difficult times in a new way. For her, a key characteristic was a sense of confidence that even the most challenging and difficult of feelings could be held within this wider container of awareness. She knew that allowing her feelings to be part of her present-moment experience in this way was not an easy road to take and that there would be no quick "fix"—but she had discovered that *anything* that arose in her experience was workable. There was something here that she could rely on.

Practising with awareness opens the way to seeing ourselves, our experience and our relationships to experience in new and radical ways. The connectedness and new learning that emerges through this process has a power to transform the ways we respond to the moments of our lives. It becomes more intuitively obvious what actions and ways of being will promote wellbeing, health and happiness.

Summary

Awareness is always present and available to us, though much of the time it is hidden from view. As soon as direct sensory perceiving of "in the moment" experience is interrupted, awareness is obscured. A gap is created between our perception of reality and the actuality of reality: "into that gap pours the mischief of our life" (Beck & Smith, 1994). We become lost in our formulations, fantasies, memories, hopes and fears about what is going on rather than seeing the direct, immediate reality of our experience. Just the process of learning how unaware we are is inherent with new learning and insight. We are clearly seeing the myriad of ways that we interrupt our ability to sustain "being mode" and how this creates our suffering. In each moment, when we open to our awareness, we are discovering a new way to "hold" and befriend our experience.

14

Working with general and specific vulnerability

The practice of mindfulness—paying attention in a particular way, without judgement—is a powerful way of "re-establishing and strengthening connectedness with our own inner landscape" (Kabat-Zinn, 2005, p. 123). This has the effect of creating well-being and greater health in ways that reach far beyond the specific effect of reducing vulnerability to depressive relapse. MBCT was originally designed to be taught during periods of remission from depression.[11] A distinctive feature of MBCT, therefore, is that participants are simultaneously gaining skills in more effectively managing their general vulnerability (traits shared by all humans), by bringing the effects of mindfulness practice into the everyday fabric of their lives, and are also learning to better manage their specific vulnerability (heightened risk of depressive relapse) (Teasdale et al., 1995; Williams, 2008). MBCT thus has the potential of offering participants a way of working with and transforming their lives in profound and far-reaching ways, as well as enabling them to work more skilfully with their vulnerability to depressive relapse. This Point addresses some aspects of the issues related to working with both general and specific vulnerability within the MBCT programme.

General vulnerabilities

Mindfulness practice and teaching illuminates our under-standing of our "general vulnerability"—the traits shared by all

11 Though see Kenny and Williams, 2007, for the use of MBCT with people who are still depressed, and Kingston et al., 2007, for the use of MBCT with people with residual depressive symptoms.

humans that tend us towards suffering. These include the use of language (which creates a tendency to separate ourselves from experience); our ability to carry out tasks, activities and thinking processes on automatic pilot (which creates the tendency to endeavour to deal with challenging emotions through habitual ruminative thinking patterns); our ability to move thought processes into the future and the past (which creates the tendency to experientially avoid the present); our physiological responses to threat (which do not discriminate between internal and external stimuli); and a general tendency to be unaware of our direct physical experience and over reliant on our cognitive processes.

MBSR, from which MBCT evolved, was developed originally to work with groups of people with a wide range of different physical and psychological challenges and illnesses. It largely focuses on inviting participants to explore their general vulnerability—the patterns and habits of mind that create struggle and extra layers of challenge as they deal with daily life and the health difficulty they are experiencing. Participants are learning to develop acceptance and compassion instead of judging their experience; to develop present-moment awareness instead of being on automatic pilot and to learn new ways to respond rather than react to experience. The particular nature of the problem that the participant is presenting with medically is not generally directly explored in the sessions. The focus is on the participant's *relationship* to it. The process of investigating these general mind tendencies within an MBSR group context leads participants to discover that whatever our particular problems, there are universal patterns that we can all recognise.

Specific vulnerability

In addition to the general vulnerability that we all share, MBCT holds that we also carry some specific vulnerability: patterns, traits or tendencies, which can be mild or considerably disabling. These are created by our particular conditioning, life events, environmental influence, illness, or genetic makeup. These specific vulnerabilities tend individuals towards such illnesses as depression or chronic fatigue. They constitute the particular places and ways in which each of us is more likely to get "stuck" or "snagged".

Targeting the learning towards specific vulnerability

The MBCT programme has a particular intention to focus the learning around developing the skills to meet vulnerability to depression recurrence. The way in which it does this is through the integration of CBT within the programme. There are two broad ways in which this happens:

1 A teaching process that makes clear, explicit links between the learning arising in the practices and their relevance to the target problem.
2 Curriculum elements that draw out particular aspects of learning that are relevant to the target problem.

The first of these is expanded further here. The curriculum elements drawn from cognitive therapy are described in Point 27.

Targeting the learning—the MBCT teaching process

Problem formulation and linking the learning to depression

MBCT is taught within an underpinning cognitive framework and understanding. Problem formulation within cognitive behavioural therapy conceptualises how different types of psychological difficulties are triggered and perpetuated. MBCT teaching thus aims to integrate the dynamic, "in-the-moment-responding" aspect of mindfulness with a clear understanding of the origins and maintenance factors of the psychopathology being dealt with. This understanding is shared with the participants (from the orientation session onwards) so that both the teacher and the participant know why they are doing what they are doing. Clear, explicit links are made throughout between the learning arising in the practices and their relevance to the target problem. The teacher weaves within the dialogue with participants, an understanding about the relationships between the person's experience, the effects of bringing mindful attention to experience and understandings about the ways that "depression mind" (in MBCT for depressive relapse prevention) is triggered and perpetuates itself. At times this is a process of facilitating participants in drawing out these connections, while at other times offering teaching that supports this integration. The learning that participants are developing through their mindfulness practice is thus particularly focused on working with their specific challenges and vulnerabilities. The teaching challenge is to connect this understanding with the direct experience of the participants so that it is integrated experientially.

Summary

The skills that enable one to better manage vulnerability can be gained through mindfulness training. The generic aspect of the training enables MBCT participants to take the programme during a period of remission and still to have plenty of "in-the-moment challenge" to practice new skills on. They can then apply their new skills to their vulnerability to depression when this is needed. The targeted nature of MBCT teaching and learning enables participants to relate their new skills to the management of their specific vulnerability.

Teachers of MBCT need to be competent in working with both general vulnerability through the medium of mindfulness training (this requires a considerable depth of experience in mindfulness practice, understanding and teaching) and also with working with specific vulnerability (this requires experience and training in working with the diagnostic conditions for which the programme is intended).

15

The MBCT evidence base

The initial MBCT research trial (Teasdale et al., 2000) was the first multi-centre randomised control trial (RCT) of a mindfulness-based clinical intervention (Teasdale, 2006). As such it broke new ground and has certainly been part of the process of stimulating widening interest in the potential for mindfulness-based approaches in clinical settings.

The first trial of MBCT (Teasdale et al., 2000)

This three-centre clinical trial of MBCT was interested in answering the primary question: does MBCT when offered in addition to "Treatment As Usual" (TAU) reduce rates of relapse in depression? One hundred and forty-five patients (who were currently in remission, had previously experienced at least two previous episodes of depression and had not taken anti-depressants for the three months before entering the trial) were recruited and randomly allocated to either the MBCT treatment group or TAU. Patients were followed up for the year after their treatment in either the MBCT group programme or an equivalent eight-week period in TAU.

The key results of this initial RCT were as follows:

- For patients who had suffered three or more episodes of depression the MBCT treatment almost halved the rate of relapse over the following year as compared with the control group receiving TAU (66% relapse rate in the control group and 37% relapse rate in the MBCT group).

- For patients who had suffered only two previous episodes of depression, there was no significant difference in the rates of relapse between treated and non-treated patients.
- The course was delivered in a group setting and so the benefit of the MBCT treatment was achieved with an average investment of less than 5 hours of time per patient.

The differential treatment effects between those with a history of three or more episodes and those with only two episodes led to some interesting questions, which were investigated in a second MBCT trial.

The second trial of MBCT (Ma & Teasdale, 2004)

A second trial was conducted in which 75 patients were recruited on one site. This trial was primarily interested in investigating:

- whether the positive results observed by Teasdale et al. (2000) for people with three or more episodes of depression could be replicated;
- whether the results observed by Teasdale et al. (2000) for people with two or less episodes of depression (in which mindfulness did not reduce relapse) would be replicated; and
- whether MBCT is specifically effective in reducing relapse in people who experience depression that is triggered by autonomous internal processes rather than relapse that is triggered by stressful life events.

The results of this trial demonstrate strikingly similar findings. MBCT more than halved the relapse rates for people with three or more episodes (36% relapse in MBCT group; 78% relapse in TAU group). Again in the group of people with two previous episodes of depression, the difference in relapse rates between the MBCT group and the TAU group was not significant.

The results of these two trials suggest that MBCT can be effective in significantly reducing the relapse rate of people who have experienced three or more episodes of depression. MBCT is now cited by the UK's National Institute for Health and Clinical Excellence (NIHCE) as a recommended treatment for people who are "currently well but have experienced three or more previous episodes of depression, because this may significantly reduce the likelihood of future relapse" (NICE, 2004, p. 76).

Ma and Teasdale (2004) carried out further investigation to determine the potential reasons for the differential effect between those with only two episodes and those with three or more. The findings indicated that the two groups of patients tended to be different populations and therefore had different pathways to depression. The group with two episodes tended to have had normal childhood experience and their depression was preceded by difficult major life events; while the group with three or more episodes tended to have had difficult childhood experience and earlier onset of depression. This suggests that the number of episodes itself may not be the critical difference between those who found MBCT helpful and those who did not. Only further research will be able to clarify whether MBCT is most effective in treating those whose pathway to depression was an early onset first episode following a difficult childhood and adolescence.

Further MBCT research and development

Research is in progress investigating further the relapse prevention in depression effects of MBCT:

- Mark Williams and colleagues (Williams et al., 2006b) are investigating the application of MBCT to people with a history of recurrent suicidal depression. MBCT is being compared to a psycho-educational eight-week programme and treatment as usual. The research is asking whether MBCT is effective in reducing the recurrence of depression in this group and if depression happens whether it reduces the suicidal aspect of the depression.

- Willem Kuyken and colleagues in Exeter, UK (Kuyken et al., in press) recruited 123 people with a history of recurring depression. Half the group participated in an MBCT course while tapering their antidepressant medication and half the group continued on antidepressants. The findings suggest that MBCT provides an alternative and cost-effective approach to antidepressants in terms of helping people to stay well.

- Zindel Segal and colleagues in Toronto are conducting a randomised control trial comparing MBCT with continuation antidepressant treatment or placebo to see whether patients who participate in MBCT are as protected against relapse as patients who stay on their medication.

- Norman Farb and colleagues (Farb et al., 2007) are using fMRI to study affect regulation following MBCT training. The investigation is asking whether the metacognitive skills for working with negative affect that patients learn in MBCT change the neural processing of sad moods.

Current research and development work is in progress investigating the adaptation and application of MBCT in other clinical arenas such as chronic fatigue syndrome (Surawy, Roberts, & Silver, 2005); oncology (Ingram, 2005); treatment resistant depression (Kenny & Williams, 2007); between episode functioning for people with bi-polar disorder (Williams et al., 2007a) and for residual depressive symptoms (Kingston, Dooley, Bates, Lawlor, & Malone, 2007).

Summary

MBCT is a cost-effective group treatment, which has been shown to halve the likelihood of depressive relapse in the year following treatment for people who have experienced three or more previous episodes of depression (Ma & Teasdale, 2004;

Teasdale et al., 2000). The approach is most effective in preventing relapse that comes about even without a current major life difficulty. This is consistent with the intervention causing a disruption of autonomous, relapse-related ruminative processes. The evidence base for MBCT is growing, and should be seen within the context of the rapidly developing MBSR research field, for which there is not space here, which demonstrates positive effect sizes for a range of conditions (see Baer, 2003, for a review).

Part 2

THE DISTINCTIVE PRACTICAL FEATURES OF MBCT

16

Course content and structure

The overall shape of the programme

The general shape of the MBCT programme is eight weekly 2- to 2.5-hour-long sessions preceded by a pre-course orientation and assessment session (see Point 18 for further details of this). There is a structured schedule of home practice, which involves 45 minutes per day of a formal mindfulness practice, some daily life informal practices and some recording of observations of experiences. Many programmes include a day of guided mindfulness practice during week six, which offers participants a sustained experience of mindfulness practice.

There is a general emphasis in the first half of the programme on learning to bring attention to "internal" experience and seeing what happens in this process. In the second half of the programme there is an emphasis on the application to life challenges of understandings that are emerging through the mindfulness practices.

The learning is supported by session handouts[12] and recordings of the mindfulness practices for each participant to take home.

The shape of the sessions

Other than in week one, each session starts with a formal practice (body scan, mindful movement or sitting meditation practice). Following this, the experience of the practice and

---

12 See Segal et al., 2002, *Mindfulness-Based Cognitive Therapy for Depression: A New Approach to Preventing Relapse*, for versions of the session handouts, which can be photocopied.

then of the home practice is explored and discussed in the particular way that is characteristic of mindfulness-based courses (see Point 28 for further details on this process of investigative dialogue between participants and teacher). There is then generally a group exercise or exploration, which draws out and investigates the theme of the week. Didactic elements and contextual information, which link the experiential learning to daily life and life challenges, are integrated throughout the teaching process. Short mindfulness practices such as the Three Minute Breathing Space (3MBS; see Point 23), mindful stretching or walking (see Point 21) are interspersed within the other elements to support participants and the teacher in reconnecting to an awareness of direct experiencing. Stories and poetry are read, which speak to the themes of the session and offer alternative doorways into new learning and perspectives. Time is given at the end of the session to laying out the home practice schedule for the following week. Each session closes with a short mindfulness practice.

There is an intention throughout the teaching to bring mindfulness to the process. Primarily this is conveyed through the teacher embodying the attitudinal qualities of mindfulness— acceptance, kindliness and gentle non-striving along with bringing a spirit of genuine curiosity and investigation to the process (see Point 30).

The content of the eight-week MBCT programme is laid out on the following individual pages in table form. As indicated, the programme elements are described in future Points. Many clinicians are now appropriately adapting the programme structure to suit their particular context and client group. It is important in this process of adaptation not to lose sight that over the years there has been much thought, research and clinical practice to evolve the current form of the eight-session mindfulness-based programme. When considering adapting the programme, it is well worth making changes from a place of familiarity with the programme in its original form so that the effects of any changes can be clearly perceived.

Week 1: Automatic pilot	
Practices in session	Eating a raisin with awareness (Point 19)
	Body scan meditation (Point 20)
Exercises in session	Group forming—setting up the ethos of the course and the group boundaries; participants introducing themselves to the group (what brought me to this course, what do I want from it)
Home practice	A 45-minute body scan meditation
	Bringing attention each day to carrying out a routine activity such as having a shower (Point 25)
	Eating one meal mindfully during the week (Point 25)

Week 2: Dealing with barriers	
Practices in session	Body scan meditation
	Ten minutes of mindfulness of breathing (Point 22)
Exercises in session	Thoughts and feelings exercise (Point 27)
Home practice	A 45-minute body scan meditation
	Ten-minute mindfulness of breathing
	Bringing attention to a different routine activity
	Keeping a daily record of the experience of a pleasant event (Point 26)

Week 3: Mindfulness of the breath (and the body in movement)

Practices in session	Mindful movement (Point 21) "Stretch and Breath practice"—standing mindful stretches, followed by sitting meditation focusing on awareness of breath and body. This can begin with a short mindfulness of "seeing" or "hearing" practice Three Minute Breathing Space (Point 23)
Exercises in session	Exploration of pleasant experiences calendar—or can be explored alongside unpleasant experiences calendar in week four (Point 26)
Home practice	Stretch and Breath practice on days 1, 3 and 5 Mindful movement practice on days 2, 4, and 6 Keeping a daily record of the experience of an unpleasant event (Point 26) Three Minute Breathing Space three times each day

Week 4: Staying present	
Practices in session	Five-minute mindfulness of seeing or hearing
	Sitting meditation (awareness of breath, body, sounds, thoughts and choiceless awareness) (Point 22)
	Three Minute Breathing Space—introducing it as a coping practice for use at times when things feel difficult
	Mindful walking
Exercises in session	Exploration of unpleasant experiences calendar
	Defining and exploring of the "territory" of depression—or alternate focus for the group, e.g. chronic fatigue, stress, etc. (Point 27)
Home practice	Sitting meditation
	Three Minute Breathing Space—Regular (three times a day)
	Three Minute Breathing Space—Coping (whenever you notice unpleasant feelings)

Week 5: Acceptance and allowing/letting be

Practices in session	Sitting meditation—awareness of breath and body; emphasise noting how we react to whatever thoughts, feelings and body sensations arise; introducing a difficulty within the practice, and exploring its effects on body and mind (Point 22) Three Minute Breathing Space
Exercises in session	Read *The Guest House* poem by Rumi and explore themes with group Exercise exploring habitual patterns of reaction and the potential use of mindfulness skills to facilitate greater responsiveness to present-moment experience
Home practice	Sitting meditation Three Minute Breathing Space—Regular (three times a day) Three Minute Breathing Space—Coping (whenever you notice unpleasant feelings); after the practice exploring the choice of opening the "body door"

Week 6: Thoughts are not facts	
Practices in session	Sitting meditation—awareness of breath and body—plus introducing a difficulty within the practice, and exploring its effects on body and mind Three Minute Breathing Space
Exercises in session	Moods, thoughts and alternative viewpoint exercise (Point 27)
	Beginning to develop a personal relapse signature and action plan (Point 27)
	Preparing for the end of the course
Home practice	Practicing for 40 minutes per day—work with different combinations of the three core practices; investigate using a range of shorter practices; investigate practicing with and without using CDs (exploring the development of a form of practice that can be sustained beyond the course end)
	Three Minute Breathing Space—regular (three times a day)
	Three Minute Breathing Space—coping (whenever you notice unpleasant feelings) and as a first step in taking a wider view of thoughts—opening the "thought door"
	Further reflection and work on personal relapse prevention action plan (Point 27)

Week 7: How can I best take care of myself?

Practices in session	Sitting meditation—awareness of breath, body, sounds, thoughts and emotions
	Three Minute Breathing Space plus introducing a difficulty into the practice and exploring its effects on body and mind
Exercises in session	Explorations of the links between activity and mood (Point 27)
	Generate list of daily activities and consider which feel "depleting" or "nourishing" and which give a sense of "mastery" or "pleasure". Consider ways of increasing the "nourishing" activities (Point 27)
	Identifying relapse signatures and actions to deal with the threat of relapse/recurrence (Point 27)
Home practice	Select from all the different forms of practice a pattern you will be able to continue with after the end of the programme
	Breathing space—regular and coping; after the practice exploring the choice of opening the "door of skilful action"
	Develop an early warning system for detecting relapses (Point 27)
	Develop action plan to be used in the face of lowered mood (Point 27)

Week 8: Using what has been learned to deal with future moods

Practices in session	Body scan meditation
	Ending meditation
Exercises in session	Review of early warning systems and action plans for use when the threat of relapse is high
	Review whole course—what are the things that you most value in your life that the practice could help you with?
	Discuss how to keep up the momentum developed in the formal and informal practice
	Questionnaire for participants to give personal reflections on course
Home practice	Settle with a plan of home practice that you can sustain for the next month (ideally this is reviewed in a follow-up session)

Laying out the curriculum in this way may lead to the impression that the programme content is fixed and rigid. It is important to remember that this is a guide and does not replace the moment-to-moment responsiveness to curriculum choices by the teacher within the sessions. There are, however, some elements of the programme that are essential and integral. These include the formal mindfulness practice; the emphasis throughout on bringing the spirit and essence of the attitudinal foundation of mindfulness practice into the fabric of the teaching process; and the interweaving within these of teaching, which draws out how our difficulties are created and sustained. Within all this the co-creation between the teacher and the participants of alive, responsive and meaningful learning will mean that no two MBCT courses are exactly the same.

17

Session themes

Week one: Automatic pilot

A significant part of this first session is spent on building a supportive environment for the work that will be done in the weeks ahead. The teaching process is intended to help participants in beginning to recognise the tendency that we have to be on automatic pilot and the effects this has on our lives. Participants see that simply bringing attention deliberately to an everyday object (a raisin) has the effect of changing the nature of the experience of this object. In practising the body scan participants see that purposefully moving attention to different places in the body is both a simple thing to do and yet is tremendously challenging—the mind seems to have its own ideas about where it will go!

Week two: Dealing with barriers

Participants arrive at the second session after a week of practising the body scan. Often they have felt challenged by this and exploration of their experiences further develops understanding of the themes opened out in the first session. The focus of attention on the body begins to show more clearly the reality of the chatter of the mind, plus it becomes apparent how this chatter tends to control our reactions to everyday events. A theme emerges of seeing how we add layers to the immediate direct experiences that life presents to us. A thoughts and feelings exercise (drawn from CBT) explores a particular aspect of this—how our *interpretation* of the situations we are in often determines how we end up feeling, rather than the situations themselves.

Week three: Mindfulness of the breath (and body in movement)

There is a strong emphasis on sustained practice within this session. Participants are introduced to mindful movement and to mindfulness of the breath. Coming after two weeks of practicing the body scan at home, this underpins the theme of establishing the body as a place to be with our experience. Taking the attention intentionally to the breath opens the possibility of working with it in new ways—deliberately using attention to become more focused and gathered. There is also an increasing awareness of how the mind can so often be busy and scattered despite our best intentions! Through the deepening exploration of their experience, participants become increasingly attuned to the elements that make up our overall experience in each moment—the body sensations, the thoughts and the emotions. Largely through meeting and experiencing the challenge of mindfulness practice, participants are developing an experiential understanding of the attitudinal foundation to the process—that there is no right way to experience the meditation practice; that it is possible to bring kindly acceptance to our struggles and that developing an interest and curiosity about what is arising opens up a new way of relating to things.

Week four: Staying present

With three weeks' experience of daily mindfulness practice, it now becomes possible for participants to discern some more detailed aspects of the nature of the mind. Session four draws out the way in which the mind is most scattered when trying to cling to some things and avoid others. It becomes clear that these reactive patterns take place most readily when we are on automatic pilot. This lays the ground for beginning to develop awareness of more effective ways of responding to difficult situations and experiences. Mindfulness can offer a way to stay present with experience and so enables us to view things from a different place. The time spent in getting to know the territory of depression develops a clearer understanding of the nature of the condition and enables an exploration of the relationship of mindfulness skills to this life challenge.

Week five: Acceptance and allowing

The emphasis on bringing to experience a sense of allowing things to be just as they are, without judgement or trying to make them different, opens the way to seeing how this, in and of itself, creates a new way of relating to experience. Such an attitude of acceptance can become a major part of taking care of oneself and seeing clearly what, if anything, needs to change. Within this the theme that was introduced in the previous week, of seeing the habitual patterns of relating to experience with aversion, clinging or tuning out, is further explored and seen as being the counterpoint to acceptance. Participants are guided in recognising their own familiar patterns of reacting (as contrasted with responding) to experience. These are related to both daily life and to vulnerability to depression.

Week six: Thoughts are not facts

The theme that thoughts are merely thoughts and that we have the choice not to act on them, engage with them, or take them personally has been implicit throughout but is now emphasised explicitly. This session draws out the way in which negative moods and the thoughts that accompany them, become the "lens" through which we see our experience. The process of recognising recurrent patterns of thought can help us to stand back from them without necessarily needing to question them and seek alternatives. However, having gained this wider perspective on our thinking process, we can choose to work with them cognitively, with an attitude of investigation, curiosity and kindness.

Week seven: How can I best take care of myself?

The underpinning theme of this session is recognising the ways in which the activities we engage in affect our mood and well-being. Bringing awareness to these effects can support us in making responsive choices about how we spend our time. These themes are linked to vulnerability to depression through seeing that learning to take action in a way that is responsive to present-moment experience is a key way of preventing future relapse. Participants learn that the fatigue of depression is different from normal tiredness. It needs increased activity if only for a short time rather than rest. They are learning to use the moment-by-moment discernment offered by mindfulness to decide when to let be and when to take action. A further key learning theme within this session is that of bringing awareness to personal patterns and personal vulnerability and seeing how this can help prepare us for future difficulty. Participants learn to apply their developing awareness and discernment to recognising and developing a "map" of their own particular depression relapse signature pattern. Participants are preparing for the end of the programme.

Week eight: Using what has been learnt to deal with future moods

Participants are encouraged to perceive session eight as the beginning of the rest of their life! Much emphasis is placed on supporting participants' intentions by linking the practice with the positive changes that they may be experiencing within themselves as a result of the programme. There is a theme of exploring how to keep up the momentum and discipline without the structure of weekly sessions. Mindfulness practice is like weaving a parachute—if we weave a little each day rather than leaving it to the time that we find ourselves jumping from the plane, there is a greater chance that it will hold us.

18

Assessment and orientation

The process leading up to participation in an MBCT programme is important. It is essential to assess the suitability of the course for participants at this point in their lives, to orientate participants to what the course offers and requires, to hear about participants' expectations of the course and to help prepare them for the programme. The attitude that the participant brings to the course is a key factor affecting how she or he engages with the programme.

This process of assessment and orientation starts from the time that the potential participant is referred or makes contact, and it continues up to the very start of the course. During this time there needs to be an opportunity for the teacher and potential participant to sit down together and mutually discover and assess whether the course is likely to be helpful at this time in the person's life.

What brings you here?

The dialogue begins with opening an invitation to the participant to share some of the personal story that led them to consider taking the course. Listening to the challenges that the participant is experiencing in their life and how their particular patterns of difficulty tend to emerge is important. A key question to have in mind is whether this is a suitable time for the person to be engaged in an MBCT programme. The course itself is challenging and tends to increase the level of intensity experienced. Generally speaking, the course may be best not taken when the person is experiencing strong life changes, significant turmoil or acute challenge.

Describing what the MBCT programme is about

Potential participants need to be informed about the course so that they can make a clear choice to engage with the programme. Finding fresh alive language to convey the spirit of the programme in ways that resonate with the person is a key challenge. Once participants have embarked on the programme, we will be inviting them to explore what we are teaching through mindfulness practices and exercises. From this experiential basis the learning is developed. Before the course starts we have to do this the other way around—we need to find ways of *describing* what the programme is intending and how this is approached. Given the subtle nature of what we are cultivating this is not easy—stories and metaphors are tremendously helpful with this.

There is a paradox inherent within the approach, which we are learning to inhabit rather than resolve. Participants naturally come wanting things to be different but rather than helping us to get somewhere else, the course will be teaching us how to be more fully where we already are! Most people are familiar with strategies involving tackling problems head on. It is important to convey that we will be exploring a different way to work with the difficulties we are faced with in life. This will not involve directly addressing or talking about the problems themselves—it will involve investigating how we are in *relationship* to them. It is helpful to make this personal by connecting the description of the ways in which MBCT *tends* to have its effects with the sorts of challenge that this person is facing. It can be useful, too, to offer some information about the evidence base for the approach. As ever, there is a fine balance here between, on the one hand, supporting the participant in committing and aligning themselves with the course and, on the other, not giving unhelpful expectations about what the course will offer to them. As Kabat-Zinn (1990, p. 171) says: "if we have ideas about how our practice should unfold these will often get in the way".

Within the description of the course, it is also useful to give a practical description of what will happen in the sessions—the meditation practices, the group discussions and exercises. Helping the person to get a feel for the style of the course is important—it isn't a therapy group; there isn't space to talk about the history of your problems; it is a place where you will be learning new skills along with a group of others who are experiencing similar life challenges; you can choose how much you participate in the group dialogues.

Home practice

The centrality of the home practice to the programme is important to convey—if they decide to take the course they are committing to one hour of home practice each day. Participants need to hear that they will not necessarily enjoy the home practice—there are likely to be times that they experience it as difficult or boring but that, nevertheless, it will be important to persevere. It can be helpful to suggest that they approach the course as an eight-week "experiment", during which time they decide to commit fully to the process and at the end of the eight weeks they can come to their own conclusions.

The challenge of taking the course

It is important that participants are aware that the course may make things feel more intense and challenging. The process of cultivating our ability to be aware can at times be likened to tuning a radio in so that the signal is clearer and turning up the volume somewhat. This increased awareness heightens our ability to connect with the pleasures around us but it also heightens our sensitivity to life's challenges and pains. Furthermore, the process of rearranging ones daily schedule to make space for the home practice involves a major life change, which many also experience as stressful.

Priming intention and commitment

Mindfulness is underpinned by an attitude of non-striving but it does not happen accidentally. The practice requires a high degree of engaged commitment and discipline—the eight-week programme is an intensive training process. Participants need to understand that the course is about learning to do something for themselves; it involves strong engagement on their part. The programme offers a structured "container" within which this work can take place.

Summary

Ultimately, the whole process of engaging with the potential participant prior to the course is about the client aligning themselves with the course and the possibility that it holds for them. It is somewhat like launching a boat—there is a stage of careful preparation and then, at a certain point, the boat takes to the water—the learning begins.

19

Eating a raisin with awareness[14]

The first practical introduction to mindfulness practice in session one of an eight-week mindfulness-based programme is eating a raisin slowly and with deliberate attention. This intentionally conveys the message that meditation is not about unusual or mystical experiences but about the ordinary in life.

The teacher moves around the group with a bowl of raisins and, using a spoon, gives one to each participant. They are invited to let go of their knowing that this is a raisin and to see it "fresh", much as a child first encounters experience. Bringing an attitude of curiosity and interest participants are guided in exploring the raisin through each of their senses: seeing it from different angles, noticing how the light catches it, penetrates it, throws shadows on it; feeling it with the fingers and lips and then with the tongue and teeth; smelling it and perhaps noticing the anticipatory build up of saliva; listening to the sounds created by moving it between finger and thumb near the ear; and then, eventually, putting it in the mouth; biting into it; and eventually chewing and manipulating it; tasting it—seeing how the taste buds perceive differently in various parts of the mouth and sensing the remaining flavour once the raisin has eventually been swallowed. There is a strong encouragement to be awake to each aspect of experience—many of us find that food is in our mouth and swallowed before we have made any conscious choices.

---

14 Parts of this Point are drawn from *The "Eating a Raisin" Practice—Aims, Intentions and Teaching Considerations*, an unpublished handout by Mark Williams, Rebecca Crane, and Judith Soulsby, 2006a.

In the group dialogue that follows the teacher invites participants to share the direct sensory experience that occurred during the practice. Participants might be asked to notice how this experience differed from their usual way of eating raisins (often by the handful!). The teacher helps the group to gather observations about the nature of our minds, as illuminated through this experience.

Learning that comes from the raisin exercise

There are four broad areas of learning that can arise for participants:

1 Experiencing the difference between *mindful awareness* and *automatic pilot*.
2 Noticing how often we are in automatic pilot.
3 Noticing how mindful attention can *reveal* things we hadn't seen before, and can *transform* the experience itself.
4 Seeing how the mind makes rapid associations from sensory information.

Each of these areas is now considered in turn.

The difference between mindful awareness and automatic pilot

The raisin practice offers the first *experiential* teaching of what mindfulness is. The teacher invites participants to explore and eat this raisin in a particular way—deliberately paying attention to the feel, smell, sight, sound and taste experience created by the raisin; participants are encouraged to allow things (including the judgements of the mind) to be as they are; the teacher conveys an attitude of curiosity and a genuine interest in exploration to the "raisin eating" experience and to the group dialogue that follows.

Noticing how often we are in automatic pilot

The raisin practice introduces the theme of the first session: "automatic pilot". Often we eat completely beyond our awareness and it is so unusual to pay this level of attention to what we eat. This opens up awareness of how true this can be for many of the moments of our lives.

Noticing how mindful attention can "reveal" and "transform"

Participants discover through the raisin practice that intentionally bringing awareness to something, in a different way to usual, changes the nature of the experience:

> I usually eat raisins by the handful, without particularly paying attention to them and I was shocked at how intense the taste of one raisin was.
>
> (Sue, MBCT course participant)

Raisins are such a common and ordinary part of most people's everyday life that it is striking to realise that there is a depth to the sensual experience of them that had not been previously realised. If this is true of a raisin it is likely to be true of much of the rest of lives.

Seeing how the mind makes rapid associations from sensory information

Many participants describe how the raisin triggers associations, which are both pleasant (e.g. "I remembered the warm safe feeling of my mother cooking Christmas cake"), and unpleasant (e.g. "I felt sad when I realised how I usually eat without tasting"). The interconnection between sensory experience, mind activity and emotions begins to reveal itself. The mind makes associations so rapidly and the next moment is flavoured by the emotions being triggered by them. It becomes apparent that mental time travel can rapidly take us far away in time and place from the reality of the direct experience of the present moment, without us consciously realising that this is happening. The simple act of mindfully eating a raisin can thus begin to reveal the connection between training ourselves to be more aware and preventing depressive relapse or dealing with major difficulties in our lives.

Summary

The raisin practice and the dialogue that follows it can support participants in experientially learning several key features about the ways that we commonly experience and process our experience:

1 If we are on autopilot, we cannot see our moods begin to change or go down.
2 In each moment there are other things to be seen if we consciously pay attention. Paying attention in this investigative and open way to even the most routine activities may reveal aspects of our experience that we had not seen before and in so doing it transforms them. It becomes apparent how immediate experiencing happens through our senses; that this can only take place in the present and that much of the time we are "absent" from this and caught up in our thoughts. This is not "wrong" but is often unintended.
3 The mind is continually making associations from present-moment experience, commonly through connecting to a memory. A process of mental elaboration and story creation can be set in motion by these associations and the mind can then engage in a habitual pattern of analysing the past and worrying about the future. We are not usually aware of where this is taking us and mostly we do not *choose* where our mind goes. Through this we can see how difficult mind states might easily take hold when we are on autopilot.

20

Body scan practice[15]

> *The body is happy (like any other living being) when we pay kindly attention to it.*
>
> (Ajahn Sumedho[16])

The body scan is the main formal practice taught during the first two weeks and participants practice a 45-minute body scan at home daily (with the support of recorded guidance) for the first two weeks of an MBCT programme. It is generally practised lying down on a mat on the floor, though if this is not appropriate for the person it is fine to do it sitting in a chair. After settling, participants are first guided to attend to the movement of breath in the body and then systematically to escort attention through regions of the body, generally starting with the toes and moving up to the head. Throughout the body scan there is an encouragement to bring a flavour of acceptance and warmth alongside one of exploration, curiosity, aliveness and adventure.

The learning which comes from the body scan

During the body scan participants are learning to:

---

15 Parts of this Point are drawn from *The Body Scan—Aims, Intentions and Teaching Considerations*, an unpublished handout by Mark Williams, Rebecca Crane, and Judith Soulsby, 2006a.

16 From a talk on scanning the body at a retreat led by Ajahn Sumedho, Amaravati Buddhist Monastery, September 2004.

1   connect with the direct experience of physical sensations
     and so access an immediate, intuitive way of knowing;
2   be *intentional* about where and how the attention is placed;
3   relate skilfully to mind wandering; and
4   allow things to be as they are.

Each of these areas is now considered in turn.

Connecting with the direct experience of physical sensations

The primary intention of the practice is to cultivate the ability to bring awareness and gentle inquiry to sensations as they are, as the attention is focused on one part of the body after another. This helps to bring us into the present moment, for that is when the body is experienced—right here, right now. The body scan is cultivating the possibility of directly "being with" body sensations rather than looking at them from a distance, thinking about them or having ideas about them. In this way it can help to reverse potential disconnection from bodily experience and supports us in "feeling at home" in our bodies.

Learning to be intentional about where and how the attention is placed

The body scan helps us to learn to *aim* and *sustain* the attention (Kabat-Zinn, 2005) where we want it, and to deliberately *engage* and *disengage* it as we move attention through the body. We learn that we can move the attention from a narrow angle focus (e.g. detailed attention on the sensations in the left big toe) to a wide angle focus (broad sweep of attention through the whole body). The body scan thus develops the ability to be concentrated *and* to have flexibility in the ways attention is brought to experience.

Prior to disengaging the attention from each area of the body, participants are invited to imagine the breath moving into this region on an inhalation and moving out on an exhalation. Directing breath into and through different parts of the body in this way helps us to learn to use the breath as a "vehicle" for directing attention. It also sets the stage for learning, later in the course, to use this way of directing the attention towards places where intense sensations are being experienced in the body.

Relating skilfully to the mind wandering

It is natural for the mind to wander. However, we often find that we judge our thoughts and feelings as being abnormal, wrong and unacceptable. This can set off a train of internal dialogue and brooding; if this doesn't resolve things we may try to suppress our thoughts and feelings. During the body scan we are learning to deal with all these patterns in a different way— to simply acknowledge where the mind went, and to gently bring it back to where we intended it to be. The effect of repeated practice of noticing, acknowledging and returning the attention to the body is in itself important learning. We realise that we do not have to attend to our distractions, react to them, or analyse them. Furthermore, we learn during the body scan to deliberately bring a flavour of warmth towards ourselves and our minds and bodies, even in the midst of challenge and repeated mind wandering.

Allowing things to be as they are

The broad intention of the body scan is to cultivate our ability to be awake to our experience. Although it is not directly aiming to help us relax many participants come to the practice with a hope that this will be the effect. Relaxation can be the experience of many, but equally we may find that restlessness, boredom or discomforts are a strong feature. Challenging though it is when our experience does not meet our expectations, this in itself can be "grist to the mill" as it helps us clearly see the mind's common pattern of finding ourselves wanting things to be different. Practicing "being with" body sensations just as they are teaches us how all pervasive such goals are and how they create difficulty for us; it allows us to begin to learn to stand back from them and to make conscious choices about those that we want to pursue and those that can be left. We are learning about non-striving and acceptance.

Summary

Repeated practice of the body scan, and exploration of the experiences that are emerging through this, supports participants in developing some experiential understandings which are foundational to the overall MBCT learning process. Through the body scan we learn to "be with" present-moment direct experience within the body; we learn that paying attention is a skill, which can be developed through regular practice; we learn that it is possible to "wake up" more often to the times when the mind moves into automatic pilot and then to simply bring the attention back to where we intended it to be; and we learn that it is possible and OK to settle into present-moment experience just as it is, even if it is not the way we want it to be.

21

Mindful movement practice[17]

Movement practices become part of the home practice schedule in week three of the MBCT programme and are integrated within the teaching process throughout. These are "meditations in motion". The practices taught are commonly drawn from hatha yoga postures but may also be drawn from other disciplines such as qigong or tai chi, depending upon the practice experience of the teacher. The practice of walking meditation is also taught—being present with the sensations of each step, and walking for its own sake without any destination. Mindful movements are done slowly, with moment-to-moment awareness of breathing and of the sensations that arise.

The MBCT teacher gives clear and precise guidance on ways of working with physical boundaries at the beginning and throughout the practice. We are learning to use our awareness of the moment-by-moment sensory "read out" from the body as a guide in making responsive choices within the practice—how long to hold a stretch, whether to move more deeply into it or ease back from it, whether and how to adapt it, or maybe not to do it at all.

Learning that comes from mindful movement

1   (Re)learning how we can bring attention to and be present with bodily experience.

---

17 Parts of this Point are drawn from *Mindful Movement—Aims, Intentions and Teaching Considerations*, an unpublished handout by Rebecca Crane and Judith Soulsby, 2006.

2 Experiencing awareness of the body in motion.
3 Embodying life experiences and processes through movements and postures.
4 Seeing our habitual tendencies played out.
5 Discovering new ways to work with intensity.
6 Experiencing working with present-moment acceptance.

Each of these is now considered in turn.

(Re)learning how we can bring attention to and be present with bodily experience

As with the body scan and the sitting meditation, the intention
in the movement practices is to learn that we can stay close to
the actuality of experience in each moment when we remain
open to body sensations. This "grounds" us into the felt
experience of the body and so directs us away from an unhelpful focus on ruminative thinking processes. Many participants
find that the sensations created during the movement practices
offer a more tangible way to feel sensory experience. They can
often experience moments of remembering and reconnecting
with the sense of being embodied (mind and body connected).
This offers glimpses of wholeness and a related sense of new
possibilities in one's life.

Experiencing awareness of the body in motion

Mindful movement practice can offer a bridge between practice
experience and daily life by creating a felt experience of awareness of movement in the body. This can then be brought to the
everyday experience of moving through one's day. Mindful
walking is especially useful for feeling the connection between
practice and daily life.

Embodying life experiences and processes through movements and postures

A felt experience of working with processes within the movement practices can offer parallels to daily life. For example:

- Balancing poses—experiencing that balancing does not happen through staying still, but through constantly recovering oneself. Similarly in life, creating balance is a process rather than an end point that we achieve.
- Transitions—the phases in the practice between postures when one is moving from, for example, lying to sitting or standing to lying, offer the possibility of practicing being in the present with a future intention. Many times in daily life we lose awareness of the present while in transition because we are focused on where we are heading rather than the process of getting there.

Positioning our body in certain ways on purpose has immediate effects on our mental and emotional state. For example:

- Standing in an erect and dignified posture without being stiff (sometimes known as the "mountain posture") offers a felt experience of "holding one's own" and "taking a stand" in life, of approaching life with a sense of inner dignity, respect and of feeling empowered.
- Curling the body up on the floor (sometimes known as the "child posture") offers a felt experience of quietening the mind, resting and protecting oneself.

Seeing our habitual tendencies played out

Engaging in the movement practices in this slow, aware and awake way gives space to see the unconscious habits that form the backdrop for how we engage with much of our lives. For example:

111

- Seeing the effects of "trying"—experiencing how often we tense up parts of our body that are not actually engaged in what we are doing in the present moment. Over time this tension can become habitual and entrenched.
- Seeing "doing mode" in action—it is easy to engage with this more active form of practice with a "doing mind", wanting to achieve certain things, hold postures a certain length of time or be competitive with ourselves and others.

Discovering new ways to work with intensity

Movement practices offer the invitation to work with physical boundaries in a particular way:

> As we carefully move up to our limits in a stretch . . . we practice breathing at that limit, dwelling in the creative space between not challenging the body at all and pushing it too far.
>
> (Kabat-Zinn, 1990, p. 96)

and

> In the process of developing a deeper awareness and sensitivity to ourselves, we are working at the limits of what we can do at any moment.
>
> (Meleo-Meyer, 2000)

Using moment-by-moment awareness of physical sensations we discover the actuality of boundaries rather than our perceptions, thoughts and feelings about them. We are learning to honour and respect what is OK for our body in each moment. All the while we are treating the exploration of boundaries as a process of discovery. The "felt" experience of working with physical sensations in these ways offers an experience of what may also be possible in relation to our thoughts and emotions. Participants can thus begin to open to the possibility of moving in close to emotional intensity in the same accepting, present-centred way that is encouraged in relation to movement in these practices.

Experiencing working with present-moment acceptance

We practice accepting our body as we find it, in the present, from one moment to the next In this way we can discover ways of honouring what is right in each moment and empower ourselves to take responsibility and make active choices that foster self-care (Kabat-Zinn, 1990).

Summary

Coming after two weeks of practising the body scan, many participants take pleasure in this more active form of practice introduced in week three of the MBCT programme. Through repeated practice of the body scan, they are often beginning to "feel into" the experience of being present with sensations. The introduction of movement practices offers an opportunity to practice this while in motion. This supports the integration of practice into daily life.

22

Sitting meditation practice[18]

The practice of sitting meditation is taught in a graduated way from week two onwards (see Point 16 for an outline of this). Participants are invited to sit either in a chair or on the floor on a cushion or meditation stool and to consciously bring the body to a posture that is both upright and relaxed. This offers a "felt sense" or an embodiment of the internal qualities that are being cultivated—an alert and relaxed awareness. The teacher offers clear guidance on which aspects of experience to bring attention to. This is integrated and interspersed with guidance on ways of working with mind wandering and invitations to cultivate the attitudinal qualities of mindfulness while doing the practice. Attention is deliberately placed on different aspects of experiencing in the sitting meditation—mindfulness of the sensations of breath movement, of body sensations, of thoughts and emotions, of the full range of experience without directing the attention to any particular focus (sometimes termed choiceless awareness) and of the experience of bringing to mind a current difficulty or challenge.

Learning that comes from the sitting meditation

The practice encourages learning in the following areas:

1 Further developing the ability to "be with" experience within the body.
2 Learning to bring the attitudinal qualities of mindfulness to experience.

18 Parts of this Point are drawn from *Sitting Meditation—Aims, Intentions and Teaching Considerations*, an unpublished handout by Mark Williams, Rebecca Crane, and Judith Soulsby, 2006a.

3   Learning to settle and calm the mind.
4   Developing a new relationship with experience.
5   Understanding how the mind operates.

Each of these areas will now be considered in turn.

Further developing the ability to "be with" experience within the body

At the beginning of the sitting meditation we narrow attention to specific details of experience such as sensations of the contact of the body with the chair or the movement of breath in the body. This takes up the attentional capacity and so offers less opportunity to get "lost"; it facilitates disengagement from the doing mode of mind activities and opens the way to cultivate a being mode of mind.

During sitting meditation we are using awareness of the body to tune into the "felt sense" of experience and so are developing a direct connection with the ways in which the mind reacts to events and stimuli with a "read out" of pleasant, unpleasant and neutral. We are cultivating the ability to be aware of the tendency to react by pulling away from or pushing towards stimuli that habitually occur. Reactions to unpleasant experience will often be accompanied by impulses of urgency, or by contraction, bracing and tightening. They represent our deep history: the ancient evolutionary tendencies we have inherited that prepare us for action.

In MBCT there is a particular interest in noticing reactions of aversion. During weeks five, six and seven participants are invited to bring to mind a current difficulty during the sitting practice (either arising from within the practice, or a difficulty being experienced in everyday life) and to work with the "felt" experience of this. This involves directly experiencing the physical sensations (whether of physical or emotional origin) arising in connection with the difficulty. This is one way to help reduce mental proliferation and to "ride the waves" of powerful internal experiences, while neither being overwhelmed by nor suppressing them. The intention is to open the possibility to choose to respond to aversive reactions in a new way—with acceptance rather than struggle.

Learning to bring the attitudinal qualities of mindfulness to experience

There is an intention throughout the sitting meditation to infuse the practice with a sense of acceptance, gentleness and curiosity. We are learning to attend with kindness and compassion—a sense that "it is OK not to feel OK". We are learning to be interested, curious and engaged in our experience. Waking up to what is happening in our body-mind system creates a shift in perspective: it enables us to turn towards rather than away from our experience and so reverses the habitual tendency to avoid that which we don't want.

Learning to settle and calm the mind

In the sitting meditation we are further developing skills in paying attention on purpose—we are learning how to gather and concentrate the mind. Cultivating an ability to settle the mind sets the stage for bringing mindful attention to a wider range of experience. Within this we are learning to consciously widen and narrow the focus of attention. For example, the transition from mindfulness of breath to mindfulness of sensations throughout the body is an expansion of attention.

Developing a new relationship with experience

An intention of all mindfulness practice is to develop a "de-centred" relationship with experience. During the sitting meditation we are cultivating this possibility of being directly and intimately present with sensory experience while *knowing* that this is what we are doing and therefore not being lost inside it. In so doing we are learning to "receive" experience as it is, as distinct from our perception and interpretation of it. Learning to de-centre from our thoughts and feelings allows us to relate *to* them rather than *from* them. The more spacious quality of mind that allows this wider perspective reduces the power of thoughts, which we can now experience as being "just thoughts" rather than facts and not therefore requiring our identification with them.

Understanding how the mind operates

Repeated experience of the sitting meditation opens the way for a deeper appreciation of the nature of the mind. We come to know *from the inside* that everything is in a state of flux and change. We see recurring patterns of actions and reactions of the mind (thoughts and emotions) and the body (impulses, aversion and contraction). We see and experience how things shift, move, change and recur within our body and mind. Regular experience of practicing in this way offers the possibility of recognising the underlying patterns and processes that drive the content of our experience. Loosening our habitual focus on the content of our experience (the things our thoughts are telling us or the throbbing pain in our back) sidesteps our tendency to ruminate or suppress.

Summary

The sitting meditation practice builds on the foundation of learning developed during the body scan and mindful movement. As well as acknowledging the arising of thoughts and emotions within the field of awareness and then returning the primary attention to the breath, there is now an explicit invitation to work directly with them through coming to an awareness of the body sensations that are associated with them. Similarly, there is an explicit invitation to turn towards the experience of challenge or intensity as it is being felt in the moment. As with other formal practice sessions during an MBCT class, each sitting meditation is followed by a period of dialogue between the teacher and the participants to facilitate and integrate the learning that is arising.

23

The Three Minute Breathing Space[19]

The Three Minute Breathing Space is a "mini-meditation" that encapsulates the essence of the entire course and also elements contained within the longer sitting meditation. Its key intention is to support the integration of practice within the fabric of day-to-day life.

The Three Minute Breathing Space (3MBS)

There are three steps to the practice:

1 *Awareness*—step out of automatic pilot, recognise and acknowledge one's current experience;
2 *Gathering*—bringing the attention to the sensations of the breath in a particular place in the body; and
3 *Expanding* the attention into the body as a whole using the particular sensations of the breath as an anchor, while opening to the range of experience being perceived (Segal et al., 2002).

The use and application of the 3MBS is built in a structured way through the eight-week programme:

• *Week three*: Practice the 3MBS three times per day at pre-programmed times.

---

19 Parts of this Point are drawn from *The Three Minute Breathing Space in MBCT—Aims, Intentions and Teaching Considerations*, an unpublished handout by Rebecca Crane, Mark Williams, and Judith Soulsby, 2007.

- *Week four*: Practice the 3MBS three times per day at pre-programmed times, plus as a "coping" practice whenever unpleasant feelings are noticed.
- *Week five*: Practice the 3MBS as described for week four with an additional element to the process—that of adding after Step 3 a sense of opening to any difficulty that may be present after the practice, using the "Body Door" (awareness of sensations) as a support.
- *Week six*: Practice the 3MBS as described for week four with an additional possibility, after Step 3, of exploring opening the "Thought Door" by "making a deliberate decision to relate differently to your thoughts" (Williams et al., 2007b, p. 202).
- *Week seven*: Practice the 3MBS as described for week four with an additional possibility of using the breathing space to open the "Door of Skilful Action" (Williams et al., 2007b, p. 202). The aim here is to use the 3MBS as a way to reconnect with an expanded awareness and then to open to the possibility of taking some considered and conscious action.

Learning that comes through the 3MBS

The practice supports learning in the following ways:

1 Generalising the practice to everyday life.
2 Developing flexibility in placing attention for different effects.
3 Accessing different ways of relating to experience in daily life.

Each of these is now considered in turn.

Generalising the practice to everyday life

The 3MBS is an important part of supporting the integration of the learning and experience of the formal practices into daily life. It offers a reminder of the wider perspective, which may have been experienced in the longer practices, and a practical vehicle for applying the programme learning to difficulties as they arise. It brings the possibility of inquiring into the nature of the patterns of the mind within the fabric of everyday life when the chance of the mind operating in automatic pilot is high. Often the continuity of awareness within the body is lost in daily life and the 3MBS offers an opportunity to reconnect with this important source of information about oneself.

Mindfulness practice teaches us that the nature of our mind in one moment affects our thoughts, emotions and behaviour in the next. The 3MBS opens the possibility of acknowledging more fully the experience of *this* moment, so that this wider awareness can inform how one works with the next moment of present awareness. This becomes explicit when participants explore using the 3MBS as a response to challenging experience.

Developing flexibility in placing attention for different effects

Throughout the programme, participants are learning to develop flexibility and intentionality in the ways that they engage their attention. Each part of the 3MBS has a particular intention and effect.

In Step 1 of the 3MBS, wide-angle attention is used to acknowledge what is present in the mind-body system. This allows us to stop what we are doing and, by taking a broad sweep of awareness through our internal experience, we are able to feel what and how we are experiencing. Along with the intentional adoption of an upright posture or bringing attention to whatever posture we find ourselves in, this whole process has the effect of supporting us in stepping out of automatic pilot and in turning towards our experience.

In Step 2 of the 3MBS, we use narrow-angle attention to gather and anchor to breath sensations and therefore to steady and settle the mind into the present moment. This process of binding the attention strongly to a detailed and particular aspect of tangible experience helps to interrupt and disengage us from ruminative mental activity.

In Step 3 of the 3MBS, we return to wide-angle attention to simultaneously anchor ourselves in the present and to open to a wider perspective of experience. We do this through keeping in touch with the sensations of movement of breath in the body, while simultaneously expanding the attention into wider bodily experience. This allows the opening into a more spacious awareness: an awareness that acknowledges what is being held in one's experience more broadly while keeping in touch with an anchor into the present moment. There is a particular intention here to infuse the attention with a sense of acceptance.

Accessing different ways of relating to experience in daily life

Developing our ability to "turn towards" experience is central within the MBCT programme. The 3MBS, with its explicit focus on acknowledging the present moment and an encouragement to use it in times of difficulty, is intended as a key practical support in developing the confidence and skills to turn towards difficulty as it arises. When we are in a constricted mind space it is easy to forget that there is a range of choices about how we can work with experience. The 3MBS can help us to enter a wider perspective in which we can perceive these choices. Segal et al. (2002) use the image of the 3MBS being like opening a door, revealing a number of further doors that we can choose to open.

Summary

Three minutes is a nominal time—the key learning that the 3MBS is facilitating is realising the potential we have to reconnect with our direct experience within the fabric of our daily lives. The three-step sequence offers a structure that facilitates a connection with our internal experience, anchoring the attention in the present and then accessing a wider awareness before stepping back into the activity of the day.

24

The importance of home practice

Is it not wise to reserve our use of the doing mode for those areas of our life in which it is a skilful, effective response and instead put more of our energies into the cultivation of being?

(Williams et al., 2007b, p. 213[20])

The body scan, sitting meditation, mindful movement and Three Minute Breathing Space practices are all examples of "formal" mindfulness practice. By this is meant that in order to practice them, we deliberately set aside some time (even if it is just three minutes!) away from the activity of the day to practice cultivating awareness. Participants in an MBCT course engage in a rigorous home practice schedule. For eight weeks they are committing to 45 minutes of formal mindfulness practice each day.

Why practice?

In part when we practice mindfulness, we are engaging in a process of investigation and discovery, and in part we are learning new skills. Neither of these can happen on a conceptual level; they both need a personal and active engagement in the process. The investigative process becomes alive and meaningful when we see what we are learning about in action in our own minds and bodies. While learning a new skill such as

20 Williams et al., 2007b, *The Mindful Way Through Depression: Freeing Yourself From Chronic Unhappiness*, New York: Guilford Press, p. 213.

playing a musical instrument or drawing, our teacher can tell us "about it" up to a point but, ultimately, if we are to actually develop the skill, we have to engage in regular practice. If the learning is to come alive and make a difference in our lives this is also true of mindfulness practice.

The aspect of mindfulness practice as a process of investigation requires that we set things up in a particular way. The doing mode of mind habits and tendencies that we are exploring are so strongly a part of our make-up that it requires some very particular conditions to enable us to view them clearly. One way of looking at this is that when we settle for a formal meditation practice, it is as if we are setting up a laboratory. Before running an experiment a scientist would spend time preparing the ground and calibrating instruments. In the same way when we practice mindfulness, we spend some time carefully setting ourselves up in the way that will give us the best possible opportunity to have a window through which we can experience and see the patterns of our mind. So, we take time to prepare the room; we ensure as best we can that there will be no interruptions; we minimise external distractions by closing the eyes or having a soft gaze on the floor in front of us; we settle into a position that embodies the qualities that we are cultivating; and we clarify our intention to allow things to be as they are, to be awake and accepting. We then start the meditation session with a deliberate focus of attention on a "narrow-angle" aspect of experience, such as breath sensations in a particular place in the body. This can facilitate a calming and settling of the mind. Once we have set ourselves up in these ways for a formal meditation session, we allow what emerges to emerge.

The aspect of mindfulness as a process of learning a new skill also requires something particular—a persistent, yet gentle determination. Learning any new skill takes a certain degree of energy though this is not like the effort of will that we are accustomed to galvanising when there is a task to be completed—this sort of effort when applied to these doing mode of mind tendencies would tend to compound and add layers to them. Mindfulness practice can be nourishing and rewarding at times and at others it can be boring and frustrating. As we practice we begin to see that the learning arises not through the content of what emerges in practice but through how we become willing to stay with it and to learn to relate to it in new ways.

Finding the time to practice

Carving out 45 minutes in one's daily schedule does not happen accidentally. Jane's experience in the early weeks of participation in an MBCT course was frustrating. She had embarked on the programme with the characteristic determination with which she often engaged in new projects. She had met with her teacher and was ready for the home-practice element of the course. Her plan was to do the practice during the day while her children were at school. However, she kept finding that in the rush of getting all her jobs done in the day, it got squeezed out. She did occasionally manage to settle to do the practice in the evening once the children were in bed. By this point in the day, though, she was feeling so tired that she struggled to stay awake during the practice. She came to the next session of the programme with a sense of despondency and failure. Her teacher invited her to become curious about the experience of "getting to do the practice". They explored together the pattern of Jane's typical days—the long "to do" lists and the feeling that she couldn't give herself some time until all the chores were done. The teacher encouraged Jane to keep working with this in a playful and investigative way. Through the next week Jane experimented with practicing first thing in the morning after the children had gone to school and before embarking on the chores. The difference this small change made was radical. She discovered that this set the tone for the day that followed—rather than scurrying through the day constantly "trying to catch up with herself" as she put it, she found that she could move more steadily through her chores, and that on the whole she completed what was needed but in a way that did not exhaust her.

Like many other mindfulness-based course participants, Jane discovered that the process of rearranging her schedule to make time for the practice opened the way for an important inquiry into what we do in our days and how we approach it. Practicing mindfulness generally requires letting go of something else that we might have been doing at that time—perhaps watching television, or sleeping or doing chores. It requires each of us to look carefully at our daily rhythms and habits and the effects that they have on us.

Summary

The time spent in sessions on an MBCT course is relatively small. The crucial backbone of the course is the daily home practice. Space is always given during each session to exploring the experience arising from the previous week's home practice. All the key learning themes within the programme can emerge through this process of investigating participants' direct experience of engaging in the home practice. Learning that emerges in this way is alive, meaningful and has impact because we connect to it directly through our own experience.

25

Mindfulness practice in everyday life

If we are willing to see the whole of our lives as practice, our awareness of the moment when we are not present, coupled with out intention to awaken, bring us into the present.

(Saki Santorelli[21])

The whole intention of a mindfulness-based programme is for the learning to be of service in making a difference in the midst of everyday life. Formal mindfulness practice is vital in giving us an experiential taste of what it is that we are cultivating. Practicing mindfulness in daily life is known as "informal practice" and this is needed to bring the fruits of the practice alive where it is needed most. Detailed exploration of the effects of intentionally bringing mindfulness into the "nitty-gritty" of our lives is a particular and important characteristic of the eight-week mindfulness-based programme. As with formal practice, the integration of the practice into daily life does not happen accidentally. It is important, therefore, to be deliberate and intentional in cultivating it.

Mindfulness of routine activities

Right from the beginning of the eight-week programme, part of the home practice schedule is to intentionally bring mindful

---

21 Santorelli, 1999, *Heal Thyself: Lessons on Mindfulness in Medicine*, New York: Bell Tower, p. 32.

attention to a routine activity. Participants are asked to choose one activity to practice this on that they engage in each day—this could be something like taking a shower, brushing teeth, reading to the children, washing up, making a meal or walking to work. The encouragement is to do the activity at a normal pace and to bring a gentle fresh attention to the moment-by-moment sensory experiences that arise each time this activity is carried out during the week. The following week they are invited to experiment with being present in this way with a different routine activity.

Within each session, space is given to sharing and exploring the experience of this. The observations that emerge through this invariably point to important learning:

> I loved the feeling of closeness with my six-year-old daughter as I read to her. Usually, I get through as quickly as I can because I know how many other things I need to get done afterwards.
>
> (Elaine)

> I discovered that even the most routine of activities can be pleasurable when I'm present. I enjoyed being outside, feeling the fresh air and seeing the sky.
>
> (Jenny—describing her experience of hanging out the washing in week two of an MBCT programme)

Discovering that spontaneous moments of pleasure are more easily accessed when we are present is a profound learning. This can be true even of activities that we might previously have labelled as routine or dull. It is interesting to note that a large part of our lives is filled with such routine activities. Commonly, the tendency is to get through them with an attitude of "this is what needs to be done in order to get to where I really want to be". We can discover that in our thrust towards an imagined future possibility (for example, getting everything done and then settling down with a cup of tea), we are continually postponing the possibility of being content with what is presenting itself to us right now.

John, in week two of an MBCT programme, described his experience, each day of the previous week, of bringing mindfulness to the walk from the bus stop to his office:

> I found it really difficult—my mind was hooked on planning the day ahead. I didn't know that my thoughts were so active.

Experiencing the *challenge* of staying present while endeavouring to be mindful of routine activities can be equally revealing. Even though John's attention had kept slipping away because his mind was persistently returning to its planning activities, the *intention* he had to be mindful enabled him to become aware of what his mind was doing while he was walking to work. He began to notice the tightening around his head and neck that seemed to accompany this mind activity and was often the precursor to a headache. He became aware that generally this process of planning, anticipating and analysing was happening without him even consciously being aware that it was going on. He realised that previously he would often arrive at work without remembering the walk and yet now he was beginning to notice small details along the way. It was spring time—buds were beginning to open and the cherry blossom was out; he noticed and smiled at familiar people along the way.

Summary

Simple though they are, these small moments of "coming to" and recognising what is taking place in and around us have a radical effect. In that moment the forward drive of the doing mind has been interrupted. Bringing mindfulness into our routine activities holds the possibility of facilitating this process of disengaging from unhelpful mind states and supporting a transition into a being mode of mind. As Jane, Elaine and John discovered, connecting directly with the immediacy of what is in hand can bring some unexpected pleasures and benefits.

26

Pleasant and unpleasant experiences

We can cultivate attention in different ways. We can simply be open and receptive to how things are in this moment, or we can focus our attention towards particular aspects of our experience. In weeks two, three and four of a mindfulness-based programme there is a particular focus on investigating feelings evoked by events that we perceive as pleasant or unpleasant. This Point outlines this element of the programme and the learning that emerges through it.

Pleasant and unpleasant experiences calendar

In week two participants are asked to record their experience each day of a pleasant event using a structured calendar sheet.[22] They are encouraged to use events that occur naturally in the course of the day. These might be quite small—seeing leaves falling from a tree, greeting a friend or drinking a cup of tea. While the event is happening the invitation is to notice what is occurring: What body sensations are present? What thoughts and images are present? What moods and feelings are present? Later on, when recording the event on the diary sheet, participants are also asked to record what thoughts are present now. In week three of the programme participants are asked to do the same thing, but this time in relation to their experience of unpleasant events. Again, the invitation is to use events that occur naturally such as being caught in a traffic jam, cleaning a

---

22 See Williams et al., 2007b, *The Mindful Way Through Depression: Freeing Yourself from Chronic Unhappiness*, for the pleasant and unpleasant experiences calendar.

spill from the floor or phoning a customer help line. During the sessions the experiences from this process of observing and recording are explored.

Pleasant, unpleasant and neutral

The range of emotions that we experience is vast and complex. However, within this complexity there is a simple aspect to the way we feel. At a direct, experiential, gut level we are constantly registering our internal and external experience as pleasant, unpleasant or neutral. The learning this leads to is core within the MBCT programme. It emerges throughout the programme but the pleasant and unpleasant experiences exercise places it in the spotlight.

Learning that comes from the pleasant and unpleasant exploration

Seeing that the experience of "unpleasant" leads to aversion

During the week of recording unpleasant experiences, Geoff was struck by noticing the aversive reactions that were triggered by an unpleasant experience and how the experience changed as he paid attention to it. Sitting in a traffic jam on the way home from work was unexpected and unwelcome—he was tired and wanted to be home. As he sat there, he moved his attention through his body as he had learned in the body scan practice. He noticed tightness through the trunk of his body and how he was pushing his body upwards and forwards. He deliberately took his attention into the muscle groups involved in this and let his body soften and relax down into the car seat. He sensed himself opening up to just being there. He noticed that in some ways he was now actually appreciating the opportunity to pause between the activity of the office and the fullness of arriving home to his family. He switched off the radio to take fuller advantage of this moment of quiet.

This radical shift in orientation from one of aversion to one of being in "approach" had taken place in the space of one minute. The ripple-on effects for Geoff and his family that evening were significant. By this simple moment of "tuning in" to his feelings he had interrupted a habitual chain of reactions, familiar to us all, which runs from experiencing unpleasantness, to aversion, to contracting physically and emotionally away from this event and on to circular and negative thought cycles. Geoff also discovered that the label he gives to events as "unpleasant" or "pleasant" becomes arbitrary once he is open to experiencing his life as it is.

A key aspect here is the movement towards *befriending* what is arising in each moment. This process is part of the general movement towards encouraging us to reconnect with and accept aspects of our experience that have been marginalised and pushed to the edges. This "tuning in" and sensitising ourselves to our feelings is the opposite of experiential avoidance.

Separating the elements of experiencing

The difference between *knowing that* our experience is made up of body sensations, thoughts and feelings and actually *directly experiencing* this interplay in action is huge. George was animated in the session while describing paying careful attention to his experience and then recording it in the diary.

. . . as I was writing down what had happened later on that day, I suddenly realised how different from usual this experience had felt. Rather than these difficult feelings being like a big "blob" of challenge, I began to see all the different bits that go to make them up . . . .

Through this process he had directly felt how it was to *relate to* his experience as a collection of body sensations, thoughts and feelings rather than viewing the world from a perspective of

135

being inside them; he found that he wasn't identifying so closely with it all and was holding it much less seriously.

Seeing biases in the way we pay attention

Jenny found it easier to "capture" and record the unpleasant experiences than the pleasant experiences. Listening to others in the group describing the range of small pleasant experiences that they had recorded helped her to realise that these sorts of events were happening in her life also, but she did not pay attention to them. She began to use her developing mindfulness practice to deliberately give attention to the pleasurable aspects of her life.

Summary

The pleasant and unpleasant experiences exploration is a tool within the eight-week programme to illuminate further the ways in which we habitually relate to experience. In particular it shines the light on automatic patterns of aversion and clinging and so sets the stage for further exploration of these themes in week five.

27

Cognitive behavioural curriculum elements

There are two broad ways in which Cognitive Behavioural Therapy (CBT) is integrated within the MBCT programme: first, through a teaching process, which is informed throughout by an underpinning understanding of the ways in which depressive relapse is triggered and maintained (see Points 2 and 14); and, second, through inclusion of curriculum elements drawn from CBT. The intention underpinning the use of these exercises varies—some are used as part of the mindfulness-orientated approach to illuminate aspects of the nature of the mind and the thinking process; others are used in the way in which they were developed within CBT for depression to give information and education about depression or to support participants in developing action-orientated strategies for preventing or dealing with depression. This Point offers a brief outline of these curriculum elements under the headings of the week in which they happen.

Week two

Thoughts and feelings exercise

The primary intention of this exercise is to facilitate an understanding that "our emotions are consequences of a situation plus an interpretation" (Segal et al., 2002, p. 143). Participants are invited to settle into a comfortable position, to close their eyes and to imagine themselves in the following scenario:

> You are walking down a familiar street. On the other side of the street you see somebody you know. You smile and wave

at them. The person just doesn't seem to notice you and walks by.

(Segal et al., 2002, p. 142)

From the range of different responses to this situation among the group members it becomes clear that how we end up feeling is mediated directly by what we were thinking about this situation. The range of feeling responses that this elicits in participants is usually broad from anger, upset, guilt, shame and sadness to little feeling response. Those that tended to think, "Oh, she/he must be preoccupied today", experienced little discomfort, whereas those who tended to think, "Oh no, I must have done something awful to offend her/him", experienced considerable upset and distress. We begin to see that our thoughts create a "lens" through which we view the world. When asked whether the thoughts that would be elicited by this situation would be different if we were in a different mood the response is unanimous—yes. Participants begin to identify that if they are in a low mood, they will be more likely to interpret a situation negatively.

Week four

Learning about the territory of depression

The intention of this exercise is to offer education about the clinical presentation of depression. Within CBT there is a collaborative process that occurs in which the therapist talks openly about the condition the client is experiencing, what is maintaining and perpetuating it and how the therapy will be aiming to help them address their problems. Within MBCT the individual assessment and orientation week prior to the course is an opportunity to explore some of this with the participant (see Point 18 for further information on this) but within the class itself there is no discussion about the causes of the participant's particular problem. The MBCT curriculum does, however, give space for an important aspect of this process—the educational element. Participants are taken through a process of identifying key characteristics of the condition. This is part of enabling them to "dis-identify" with depression (to see its universal rather than personal characteristics), gain a new perspective on their symptoms, share common experiences of a condition that is isolating and hidden, develop an informed knowledge of it rather than seeing it as shameful and facilitate a recognition of relapse signatures so that they can take skilful action earlier.

Two tools are used to facilitate this process of exploring the package of thinking styles, behaviours, feelings and moods that are labelled "depression". The first is the "Automatic Thoughts Questionnaire" and the second is the "Diagnostic Criteria for Major Depression Episodes".[23] This is where, when MBCT is being adapted for other client groups, different educational material is used.

Week six

Mood and alternative viewpoints exercise

The intention of this exercise is to see that not only does what we think affect how we feel but that how we feel affects what we think. It can be worked in a number of ways. One way is to divide the group into two. One of these small groups is given version one of a scenario:

> You are feeling down because your manager has just criticised some work you have done. Shortly afterward, you see another colleague in the General Office and he or she

---

23 Both of these are available as handouts, which can be photocopied, in Segal et al., 2002, *Mindfulness-Based Cognitive Therapy for Depression: A New Approach to Preventing Relapse*.

rushes off quickly saying they couldn't stop. What would you think and feel?

The other small group is given version two of the scenario:

You are feeling happy because your manager has just praised some work you have done. Shortly afterward, you see another colleague in the General Office and he or she rushes off quickly saying they couldn't stop. What would you think and feel?

(Segal et al., 2002, p. 255)

Note that the second part of the scenario is identical but that they are each preceded by a different event. Each group generates the thoughts and feelings brought up by the scenario they are working with before coming back together to share experiences. The difference between the two groups is generally dramatic. This learning is important—the theme of the session is "thoughts are not facts" and this is illuminated in a striking way. In each moment we "inherit" the consequences of what has been our experience in previous moments. The mindfulness skills being learnt offer an opportunity to break this chain of reactivity by noticing and widening our perspective. Just remembering that our interpretations are influenced by a number of things, including past experience and current mood states, helps us to hold them a little bit more lightly—we can choose to see that they are not necessarily representations of the truth.

Cognitive ways of working with difficult thoughts

The use of the Three Minute Breathing Space is expanded in week six to encourage its use during times when thoughts are perceived as constricted or challenging. Following Step 3 participants are invited to enter the "Thought Door" by making a deliberate decision to work with thoughts differently (Williams et al., 2007b). To support this, participants are given a handout to take home listing a range of strategies drawn from cognitive therapy for working with difficult thoughts. The strategies offered are those most likely to foster a de-centred relationship (e.g. Is this over-tiredness? Is this confusing a thought with a fact?) rather than strategies that challenge the content of thoughts.

Week seven

This session acts as a gathering point for integrating newly learnt skills of pausing and discerning what is arising in the present moment, with some action-orientated CBT strategies for working with depression. The intention is to ensure that MBCT participants gain the benefit of learning these evidenced-based strategies for taking action in particular ways when depression threatens.

Learning to see the connections between activity and mood

Participants are guided in an exploration of what "nourishes" and "depletes" them in daily life; what gives a sense of "mastery" and a sense of "pleasure"; how "balanced" the varying activities of their lives are. Within this, participants might explore how to "hold" the difficult aspects of their lives. Explicit guidance is given for what to do when feeling down: first take a breathing space; then, while holding in mind "How can I best take care of myself right now?", choose what to do next with an inquiring and open mind. This might be working with thoughts in the ways discussed in week six or it might be taking action in some way. Clear guidance is given on ways to take action—as an experiment and staying present with the experience of the activity rather than being focused on outcome.

Weeks six, seven and eight

Developing a relapse-prevention action plan

Participants are guided in developing a personal and unique relapse-prevention action plan for the future. This identifies the unique patterns of emotional response and negative thinking that act as warning signals for potential relapse and incorporates personalised actions to take in the event of future depression, hopelessness and suicidal ideation.

Summary

The integration of CBT within the mindfulness-based programme is done with care and intention. The CBT elements used and the ways in which they are taught are wholeheartedly rooted within the attitudinal framework of mindfulness. Whereas in a CBT context these exercises might be used as a basis from which to move into a therapy-style process, within a mindfulness context they are used with clear intention to foster a de-centred perspective, to deepen insight into the nature of the mind, to inform about depression and to develop awareness and skills related to managing vulnerability to depressive relapse.

28

Investigating experience

> *Learn your theories as well as you can, but put them aside when you touch the miracle of the living soul.*
>
> (Jung[24])

When we practice mindfulness we are investigating and inquiring into the nature of our mind. The participatory dialogue between the participants and the teacher in a mindfulness-based course is an interactive expression of this same inquiry process. This dialogue between participants and teacher follows each practice within an MBCT class. The aim is for the teacher to embody the same spirit of openness to whatever is noticed that each participant is encouraged to take to their own moment-to-moment experience in daily life. It is a key aspect of the teaching process as it facilitates a "translation" of the direct experience arising within the mindfulness practices into learning that participants can apply in their lives.

Elements within the investigative process

The intention of the dialogue between participant and teacher in an MBCT class is to:

- Draw out whatever participants *noticed* during the practice, and by doing this encourage them to reflect on and explore their experience.

---

24 This classic quote from Carl Jung can be found on many websites, for example: www.mindmendtherapy.com.

- Work together through *dialogue about* these observations to find out what is being discovered.
- *Link* these observations and discoveries to the aims of the programme.

Figure 2 represents diagrammatically the movement of this exploration from the personal experiential process in the central concentric circle ("What was your direct experience?"), out into a personal context of learning (noticing personal patterns, seeing the effects of bringing attention to experience) and out again into exploring how all this is relevant to daily life and to working with the challenge of depression.

Rather than being linear these areas of exploration point to the various potential processes in action during dialogue between participant and teacher. The crucial point is that the conversation is rooted in the direct experience of the participant, and that, throughout the engagement, the teacher also has a connection to his or her own direct experience. The dialogue is thus informed by the teacher consciously "tuning in" to the "feel" of things within their own sensory field, within what is emerging in the co-creation between them, within the participant they are in conversation with and within the wider group. Responses arise intuitively from this "in-the-moment" awareness. Inquiry requires the teacher "to sharpen his/her ability to listen closely, allow space, refrain from the impulse to give advice, and instead to inquire directly into the actuality of the participant's experience" (Kabat-Zinn & Santorelli, 2005).

Being alive to the moment

The dialogue in a mindfulness-based course is a way of being present with another in an open, exploratory, compassionate and accepting way without a sense of "agenda". This responsive "in-the-moment" exploration is embodying a potent possibility to participants—a potential that they could bring present-moment, non-judgemental awareness alive in their own lives.

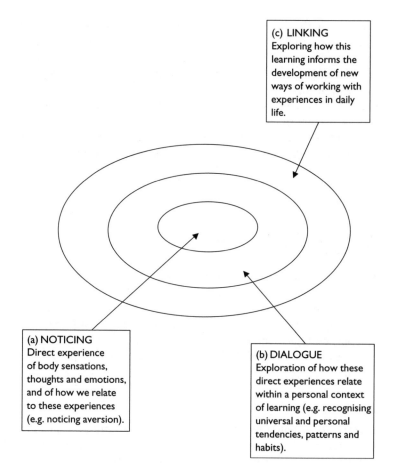

(c) LINKING
Exploring how this learning informs the development of new ways of working with experiences in daily life.

(a) NOTICING
Direct experience of body sensations, thoughts and emotions, and of how we relate to these experiences (e.g. noticing aversion).

(b) DIALOGUE
Exploration of how these direct experiences relate within a personal context of learning (e.g. recognising universal and personal tendencies, patterns and habits).

Figure 2 Layers within the inquiry process

Working with what is directly arising in the moment is therefore a necessary and powerful component of this process. As soon as a teacher prioritises conveying a "teaching point" over acknowledging and honouring what is immediate for a person or the group, an opportunity is lost. And yet there are learning themes to be conveyed. The dynamic tension of honouring the unique texture of each moment *and* teaching a curriculum is one of the many paradoxes that a skilful mindfulness-based teacher dances with. All this asks a lot of the teacher: it asks that they come to this willing to be fully human with all the vulnerability and strength that this includes. It is a tender and delicate process.

The attitudinal basis

Jon Kabat-Zinn (1990) described seven attitudinal qualities that underpin mindfulness practice, which are both the stance we bring to the practice and a consequence of it. These qualities are brought to the heart of the interactive engagements between teacher and participant in a mindfulness-based session. The qualities are described here as they relate to this process of inquiry.

Non-judging

Investigative dialogue offers an opening of kindly awareness to the stream of experience just as it is, without adding interpretation or judgement. In this way it becomes possible to see more clearly the *internal* process of adding judgement and reaction to experience.

Patience

The process of investigating experience simply works with things as they are right now and allows an understanding that change takes place in its own time.

Beginner's mind

A key intention is to spark the person's curiosity about their experience: the process at its best feels fresh and vital. It is an engaged exploration into the "how?" and "what?" of experience rather than the "why?" This supports a deliberate intention to avoid *analysing* the history and causes of what is arising. Participants are thus supported in learning to stay in the present, and to develop clarity about experience as it is right now rather than looking at it through a fog of preconceptions.

Trust

Participants are being encouraged to develop a faith in the validity of their own sensations, feelings, thoughts and intuition. During an inquiry process the teacher is conveying a sense of trust in the person's expertise in relation to their personal experience. The practice followed by inquiry thus offers a structure and a process for enabling each person to see clearly and to explore personal experience, plus an encouragement to rely on the validity of this evidence.

Non-striving

During an investigative engagement with a participant the teacher embodies an attitude of willingness to allow the present to be the way it is and for each participant to be the way they are. The process is explicitly not trying to fix problems but rather is intending to uncover an awareness of the actuality of experience, and a willingness to let it be the way it is.

Acceptance

Embodied in the process is an openness and willingness to see things as they actually are in the present moment—a way of being with the reality of experience without struggling to change it. The pain that is often felt within this process is acknowledged and "tended" through the kindly compassionate way of being offered by a skilful MBCT teacher. Many participants describe that the self-compassion and sense of goodwill towards themselves developed during the programme was kindled through the acceptant and kindly stance of the MBCT teacher.

Letting go

Mindfulness-based investigative dialogue nurtures the development of an ability to stay present and acknowledge the arising and passing of experience such as thoughts and emotions without becoming entangled in the content of it. Through this particular and deliberate way of describing and exploring *direct* experience participants are learning to let go of a habitual unhelpful focus on *thinking about* experience.

Summary

The intention of the process of inquiry or investigative dialogue is to facilitate the participants in recognising their own direct experience, in placing the experience in a context of personal understanding, in bringing new learning into conscious awareness and in connecting all this with understandings and skills that relate to working with challenges in daily life. Underlying these explicit intentions is an implicit process of enabling participants to see and experience a new way to be with their wider experience. By the end of the programme, the hope is that participants may have begun to internalise this exploratory, acceptant way to relate to life.

29

The MBCT learning environment

> *The eight-week course offered me a place where I dared to do what I needed to do for myself.*
>
> (Lynne, MBCT course participant)

A distinctive learning environment is cultivated within which to teach the eight-week mindfulness-based programme. The aspects of this that are particularly highlighted here are the theme of intentionality, the style of relational process between participants and teacher, the experiential learning process and the group context within which the learning takes place.

Intentionality

In order to set the stage for this particular form of learning, a certain sort of intention and purpose needs to be cultivated. Sustaining a commitment to a regular mindfulness practice requires a strong degree of determination, persistence and motivation. However, if this is approached in our customary way of adding "doing practice" to our "to do" lists, we are approaching the cultivation of "being mode" of mind through our "doing mode" of mind. This immediately has the effect of undermining what we are cultivating. The combination of working in non-striving ways while also being focused, clear and directional forms a paradox, which is central and inherent to approaches based on mindfulness.

Awareness itself needs no "doing" in order for it to happen—it is underlying every experience. The curious thing is that the process of bringing attention to experience does not

149

involve *doing* anything other than having an intention to stay with and open our eyes to the process. All that we *do* while we are practicing mindfulness is in the service of making way for us to learn to stop persistently *doing*. The primary thing to take care of in this process is to clearly establish an intention to be present and to turn towards experience.

The practice of mindfulness therefore encourages us to pay attention to the intention and motivation that we bring to the process. The teacher is helping participants relate the practice to a "personally valued vision" (Segal et al., 2002, p. 92). This is quite subtle and is conveyed through careful use of language (e.g. the phrase "try to keep your attention on your breath" has quite a different effect from "as best you can returning the attention to the breath each time it slips away") and through the teacher giving expression to the qualities of "non-striving" alongside "firm intention" in their entire way of being during the teaching.

Relational learning

The qualities that the teacher brings to participants mirror the qualities that they are learning to bring to themselves during the programme. The definition of mindfulness cited in Point 1 therefore describes the nature of the relationship well. Mindfulness is the awareness that emerges through paying attention to experience in a particular way: on purpose (the teacher is deliberate and focused when relating to participants in the sessions); in the present moment (the teacher has an intention to be wholeheartedly present with participants); and non-judgementally (the teacher brings a spirit of deep respect and acceptance to participants).

The other key characteristic of the relational style between participants and teacher is the sense of mutuality to the process. The processes of mind that are under investigation fall under a continuum of experience that *everyone* can relate to. There is therefore no way in which the teacher separates him- or herself from the process of investigation. In the spirit of adventure that is core to this learning style, the process of exploration within the sessions becomes a collaborative venture between all those engaged in it—there is a feeling of "co-journeying" and of a highly participatory learning process involving participants and teacher alike.

The teacher has a strong degree of responsibility to create the particular conditions for this learning to take place but beyond this the person takes responsibility for their own learning process. The intention is to empower the participant to come to know that they are their own experts. They already have a "fund of relevant experience and skills" (Segal et al., 2002, p. 92). This is conveyed in a range of ways including a strong invitation to take care of themselves within the learning process and to only follow the guidance and participate as much as feels appropriate and right to them.

Describing his experience of participating in an MBCT class some months afterwards, George emphasised the importance to him of the teacher's stance within the learning process. He had felt that the teacher was "alongside" him and his fellow participants rather than coming in as an expert and this had been significant in his own transition towards changing his relationship with himself and his experience. Rather than remaining caught up in his own personal criticism of the tangle of his thoughts, he began to see that these mind processes are a universal experience. The experience of feeling valued and attended to, just as he was in each moment, was a gradual catalyst for learning to be this way with himself.

Experiential learning

There is a movement within a mindfulness-based course from a deliberate and detailed engagement with personal experience, into a learning process that supports the participants in "translating" this direct "seeing" into learning, which they can make use of in their daily lives. Through guiding the mindfulness practices and the group exercises, the teacher is creating a series of personalised learning situations, which are then investigated. Within a mindfulness-based course, experiential learning involves developing ability to intuitively sense "felt experience" within the body and to trust the validity of what is sensed. This serves as a base from which the learning emerges. Teasdale (1999) makes the distinction between metacognitive knowledge (*knowing* that thoughts are not always accurate) and metacognitive insight (*directly experiencing* thoughts as events in the field of awareness). The suggestion is that the practice of mindfulness develops metacognitive insight, which has more potency in terms of enabling a skilful disengagement from ruminative thinking patterns and difficult emotional experience. Insights that emerge in this way can be like a "light bulb"—they illuminate understanding in a new way and have far greater impact than learning that arises through a conceptual doorway.

Learning in a group

Through engaging with the details of personal experience we come to see universal patterns. These illuminate the general nature of the human mind. The group or "class" context within which the learning happens is deliberately used to underline this. For example, when the teacher explores experience with a participant, it is a conversation with an individual within the context and implicit engagement of the group. Although the content of what is being explored will be particular to the person, the mind habits, patterns and processes that are revealed will be familiar to most. The way in which they are explored offers an embodiment of a new way of being with experience. Through witnessing each other's experience in these ways participants come to feel how normal it is to struggle in the ways that they have been experiencing. They come to sense how universal rather than personal it all is. This in itself is core to shifting participants' perspectives and stance in relation to their experience.

The group aspect to teaching and participating in an MBCT class is a significant and potent part of the experience. In many ways participants are engaging in a highly personal and internal learning process—much of the session time and all of the home practice time involves the person exploring their own experience in a solitary way. The interface of this with that of fellow participants, plus the particular way of exploration that is characteristic of mindfulness-based groups is where the learning comes alive. Given the centrality of the group within the learning process, it can be seen that the skill with which the group process is managed is of paramount significance.

Summary

The nature of the MBCT learning environment is characteristic and particular. Given the strong emphasis on each participant taking personal responsibility for their learning process, the cultivation of a supportive "container" within which this can take place is one of the prime responsibilities of the teacher. Developing the skills to create and hold this particular environment is a key focus of MBCT teacher-training processes.

30

Teaching through embodiment

> *Let the beauty we love be what we do.*
> (Rumi[25])

Teaching MBCT requires a range of competencies including skills in teaching, in working with groups, in working with the client groups for which the course is intended and in the organisational aspects of setting up groups. Although these skills would require "tuning" to the particular needs of teaching a mindfulness-based group, they can be gained in other contexts. The key distinguishing skill, which is essential for successfully conveying the essence of an MBCT course, is that of being able to teach through an embodiment of the qualities of mindfulness. This final Point therefore focuses on this area followed by an outline of a typical teacher-training pathway.

Learning to be embodied

At their heart, learning approaches based on mindfulness are environments in which participants can engage in deep explorations of the experience of what it is to be human and of investigating the way they hold this. It is challenging to articulate in words what this really means in practice yet it is easy to recognise when one is part of a teaching process that truly allows this

---

25 Barks et al. (translators), 1995, "A Great Wagon" from *The Essential Rumi*, San Francisco: Harper, p. 36.

deeper dimension to be drawn forth: the room holds a feeling of animation, honesty, aliveness, connection and presence.

A distinctive feature of mindfulness-based approaches is the consistent and strong voice from practitioners in the field emphasising that the teacher's personal practice is a crucial underpinning to the teaching process. This is a substantial demand on the life of the teacher, which moves way beyond the boundary of the workplace into every corner of their life. Some exploration of this is justified here. So, what is meant by having a personal practice and why is one necessary in order to be able to teach mindfulness-based approaches?

Recall from Point 1 that the ingredients of a personal mindfulness practice are the development of awareness (clear seeing) cultivated during formal and informal practice in daily life; the intention to underpin one's practice and life with a particular attitudinal framework characterised by warm acceptance, non-striving and curiosity; and a willingness to engage in an alive exploration of what it is to be human and of how our suffering is caused. All of this requires considerable ongoing determination and commitment in daily life, supported by contact with mindfulness teachers and periods of sustained practice in a retreat context. Although rewarding, this commitment to practice is not easy—it involves intentionally coming face to face with aspects of self that are challenging to acknowledge.

Mindfulness is not a set of techniques that one can simply learn and then sit back and enjoy the fruits. Why? Because the pervasive habits that we are seeing and working with during the practice are an inherent part of being human—on different levels and in different ways we will be exploring them and loosening their hold on us throughout our life. For those for whom mindfulness resonates, it becomes an orientation to and a way of being within one's life and the world. This does not deny that learning some elements of mindfulness as a technique or a skill holds benefit, but if its full potential is to become available it cannot be an "add on" to one's life. We ask a lot of our participants in the programme in terms of commitment to practice. A working principle for mindfulness-based teachers is that we ask as much of ourselves and that we are all students—learning and growing are life-time engagements (Kabat-Zinn, 2003).

Furthermore, it is important that participants have the confidence that the person teaching them has explored in depth the territory that they are being led into. This territory is our "being mode" of mind. In order to be able to guide others in navigating into and around it, we need deep familiarity with exploring it ourselves and with seeing how "doing mode" tenaciously reasserts itself over and over. It is through personal practice that teachers learn that the problematic patterns of mind that are the target of MBCT arise in doing mode, are perpetuated by doing mode and therefore cannot be effectively addressed by doing mode! Segal et al. (2002, p. 76) point to the challenge:

> In practice, the tendency to enter into doing mode is so pervasive (especially when one is learning a new skill such as how to "be"!) that very simple learning situations have to be set up, and the instructor has to embody being mode more or less constantly in those situations in order to facilitate entry into this mode of mind.

Mindfulness-based teachers who are predominantly teaching through "doing mode" will tend to default to seeing and working with things through their critical thinking and problem-solving mind; they will tend not to discern the patterns of mind that are the target of MBCT or be able to articulate the discriminatory processes cultivated in mindfulness. They will have a limited map of the territory of their own mind modes. Attempts to address challenges through a problem-solving mind risk reinforcing an attitude that problems are to be battled with, that they can be fixed and that once they are eliminated then everything will be alright (Segal et al., 2002). Mindfulness practice enables us to see that if one expects or wants something to arise, in one's own process or that of others, one has immediately moved beyond the present moment and into a future concept with a personal judgement attached to it. This is radically different from a full embracing and acceptance of the present moment just as it is.

A teacher who is *embodying* mindfulness has taken in, at a level that goes deeper than conceptual understanding, what it means to directly connect with and relate to experience and the world through awareness of the present moment and with acceptance. It is through this that they learn to be deeply present with participants and their difficulties without moving in to fix things; to be willing to teach through a felt knowing of their own vulnerability; to bring gentleness and compassion to themselves and the participants; to have enough familiarity with this process of being and learning to be able to trust in the unfolding of it; and to be able to articulate the subtlety of experience in a way that resonates with meaning for the participants in the group.

As this process develops the teacher becomes able to operate within this being mode of non-judgemental, present-centred awareness even in the sometimes charged and intense environment of the mindfulness-based class. The teacher's actions are thus arising from openness to this moment in its fullness and indeterminacy and to a willingness to not know the answer. This is significantly different to potentially limiting actions on the part of the teacher that are based on previous expertise, intellectualisations of the current situation or an inner wanting to do something that would help resolve the presenting difficulty.

These all sound like daunting demands . . . and in truth many, many mindfulness-based teachers would express that they don't feel ready to do this work. Yet they still "show up" in the sessions and bring with them their human frailty, their sense of incompleteness and with that their wholeness. Many, many participants express that it is this—human contact with another being who is participating in the same journey (even if the trajectory is somewhat different) that has sparked a sense of possibility and potential within them.

MBCT training processes

As can be seen from the emphasis in this Point and throughout the book, MBCT is not a small variant on CBT; it is a *mindfulness-based* learning process, which is a major discipline in its own right. Given that the transformative potential of the programme is reliant on gaining access to perspectives that arise during mindfulness meditation practice, it follows that the professional training process for MBCT teachers should also offer the particular conditions within which these perspectives can be cultivated and explored. Stated simply, MBCT training is mindfulness-practice based.

The learning trajectory that supports the teaching involves an alive and engaged inquiry into what it means to be human and so there are multiple pathways through which MBCT teachers arrive at this work. There are, however, some consistent and common threads and various training organisations (see further resources), which offer developmental processes that support the required learning. The following section offers an overview of a typical training pathway.

Foundational training

A primary "qualification" for teaching mindfulness-based approaches is that mindfulness has become a way through which we explore and engage with our experience and our life. Of course, this requires each person to test this out for themselves. Before contemplating integrating mindfulness within one's professional context, the requirement is to develop a personal mindfulness practice purely as an experiential learning process for oneself. Following this it will be possible to decide whether to take this exploration and development further.

There is a range of ways of supporting the development of a personal mindfulness practice. Although we can be tremendously inspired by reading books, ultimately it is challenging to sustain a mindfulness practice without personal contact with experienced teachers and with others who are practicing. Mindfulness teachings are generally based on meditative disciplines from Buddhist traditions, but are open to those with any faith or none. Participation in an eight-week mindfulness-based course offers a secular and "applied" engagement with the practice and it is certainly important that trainees are deeply familiar with the curriculum and process of a mindfulness-based course before embarking on teacher training.

The foundation of one's personal mindfulness practice becomes the "bedrock" of the teaching process. Learning to teach the MBCT programme in ways that allow the richness and potential of mindfulness-based learning to become accessible to the participants involves a committed engagement to this long-term personal development process. However, the experience of MBCT trainees is that the rewards of this engagement go far beyond the development of the ability to teach or integrate mindfulness within one's professional work.

Preliminary teacher training

Trainees must enter preliminary MBCT teacher training with:

- Sufficient depth of personal experience with mindfulness practice to begin the development towards teaching. This must include a regular engagement with the three main practices taught in mindfulness-based approaches (body scan, sitting practice and mindful movement practice).
- Familiarity with the eight-week mindfulness-based course structure and process.
- Training in a structured psychotherapeutic approach such as CBT.

- Professional training and experience in the context within which they plan to teach MBCT.
- Experience and skills in leading and teaching groups.

This training stage is often offered as a week-long residential training within a retreat context. This offers a container for learning, which enables participants to access and develop their "inner" practice-based exploration alongside the development of knowledge and competencies in teaching. The practice-based learning context enables the "outer" and more visible learning processes to be informed and "related to" in a mindful way.

Advanced teacher training

Following completion of preliminary teacher training, trainees enter advanced MBCT teacher training with:

- experience of having taught several MBCT courses;
- commitment to attendance on regular mindfulness-practice retreats; and
- engagement in a regular supervision process with an experienced mindfulness-based teacher.

Trainees at this level will have moved beyond the early explorations of the form and shape of the MBCT programme and curriculum, and will developmentally be at the point of exploring ways to refine their existing skills and to deepen their understanding of mindfulness as a teaching and learning process. A key overall intention is to support trainees in developing the ability and confidence to teach from the immediacy of their own experience. This tends to grow out of a depth of experience with mindfulness practice, with the teaching process and with the form of the MBCT programme. Developmentally, many teachers experience that their confidence of knowing what is needed develops to the point that they can let go of holding the teaching in a certain way and relate to the process from a wider, more embodied, creative and spacious place. This training is commonly structured as a week-long residential training within a retreat context.

Ongoing training

It is important that MBCT teachers consider the development of their personal mindfulness practice and the teaching of the programme to be a life-long learning process! There is no point at which it is completed. In order to keep sustaining their ability to teach in the ways particular to mindfulness-based programmes, they must remain engaged with processes that keep the learning alive. These include ensuring that:

- There is an ongoing commitment to a personal mindfulness practice through daily formal and informal practice, attendance on retreat and through engaging with mindfulness teachers.
- Ongoing contacts with colleagues engaged in mindfulness-based teaching are built and maintained as a means to share experiences and learn collaboratively (it is particularly helpful to arrange for colleagues to give direct feedback on one's teaching).
- An ongoing and regular process of supervision of teaching and inquiry into personal practice by an experienced teacher of mindfulness-based approaches is in place.
- Assessment of the experience and outcomes of participants in the classes using standard measures takes place.

Summary

MBCT integrates understanding from contemporary scientific, theoretical and clinical understanding with practices drawn from the 2500-year-old mindfulness meditation teaching tradition. Its success as an evidenced-based targeted clinical approach is creating an understandable demand from practitioners wanting to become "qualified" to teach. Meeting this needs to be balanced with the understanding that MBCT training processes place a strong emphasis on the trainee's study of their own inner direct experience and in their sustained commitment to nurture the mind towards wisdom, gentleness and compassion— processes that are not easily measured or assessed!

Further resources

If you are interested in taking your learning further this section offers some suggestions for further reading, websites, training organisations and retreat centres. These are primarily focused on mindfulness-based training and its clinical applications because cognitive behavioural approaches within therapy are well established and information on them is readily available.

Developing and supporting personal practice

There are many mindfulness teachers and centres from which to choose. Gaia House in Devon, UK (www.gaiahouse.co.uk) and its sister centre the Insight Meditation Society in Massachusetts, USA (www.dharma.org) teach mindfulness practice in a spirit and form that is compatible with the MBCT programme and are therefore particularly recommended.

Recordings of guided mindfulness practices are an invaluable support when meditating at home. Jon Kabat-Zinn's CDs are available through www.mindfulnesscds.com. Practices as they are used in the MBCT programme are available through the Oxford Mindfulness Centre (www.mbct.co.uk) and through the

Centre for Mindfulness Research and Practice at Bangor University (www.bangor.ac.uk/mindfulness).

Professional training

Training processes and organisations are developing rapidly. Within the UK there are three university-based training establishments that offer MBCT teacher training:

1   The Centre for Mindfulness Research and Practice within Bangor University's School of Psychology offers two master's degrees (MSc or MA): a specific programme in Teaching Mindfulness-Based Courses and a general master's in Mindfulness-Based Approaches. The Centre also offers a comprehensive Continuing Professional Development programme (www.bangor.ac.uk/mindfulness).
2   Exeter University offers a Postgraduate Diploma in MBCT (www.ex.ac.uk).
3   Oxford University offers a Master of Studies in MBCT (www.mbct.co.uk) and other MBCT training events through the Oxford Cognitive Therapy Centre (www.octc.co.uk).

The MBCT websites for North America (www.mbct.com) will give information on developments there and to some extent in Europe. The training available for MBSR also provides excellent preparation towards teaching MBCT. Further details of MBSR training opportunities are available from the Center for Mindfulness in Medicine, Health Care and Society, University of Massachusetts Medical School, USA (www. umassmed.edu/cfm).

Books

The two seminal books on MBCT are *Mindfulness-Based Cognitive Therapy for Depression: A New Approach to Preventing Relapse* by Segal, Williams, and Teasdale and *The Mindful Way*

Through Depression: Freeing Yourself from Chronic Unhappiness by Williams, Teasdale, Segal, and Kabat-Zinn. Both are invaluable—wonderfully written, informative and accessible. The former is aimed at the therapist or clinician and describes the development of the approach, the theoretical underpinnings and offers a session-by-session exploration. The second is intended as a self-help guide for those exploring mindfulness practices as a way of working with depression, but it also offers the clinician a user-friendly guide to the latest scientific understanding and a compassionate window on this work.

Kabat-Zinn's first book *Full Catastrophe Living* describes the MBSR programme in an accessible and engaging way and is essential reading for those wanting the background to the development of the clinical applications of mindfulness. He has also written *Wherever You Go, There You Are* (published in the UK as *Mindfulness Meditation in Everyday Life*), which is a wonderful support to the development of personal practice, and *Coming To Our Senses: Healing Ourselves and the World Through Mindfulness*, which offers a broad and wide ranging though deeply personal exploration of the potential for mindfulness within our lives and the world.

Selected further reading

Baer, R. E. (2005) *Mindfulness-Based Treatment Approaches: Clinician's Guide to Evidence Base and Applications*. San Diego, CA: Academic Press.

Feldman, C. (2004) *The Buddhist Path to Simplicity: Spiritual Practice for Everyday Life*. Lanham, MD: Element.

Germer, C. K., Siegel, R. D. and Fulton, P. R. (2005) *Mindfulness and Psychotherapy*. New York: Guilford Press.

Goldstein, J. (1993) *Insight Meditation: The Practice of Freedom*. Boston: Shambhala.

Greenberger, D. and Padesky, C. (1995) *Clinician's Guide to Mind Over Mood*. New York: Guilford Press.

Hayes, S., Follette. V. and Linehan, M. (eds) (2004) *Mindfulness and Acceptance: Expanding the Cognitive Behavioral Tradition*. New York: Guilford Press.

Kornfield, J. (1994) *A Path with Heart*. New York: Bantam.

Nhat Hanh, T. (1991) *The Miracle of Mindfulness*. London: Rider.

Rosenberg, L. (1999) *Breath by Breath: The Liberating Practice of Insight Meditation*. Boston: Shambhala.

Salzberg, S. (1997) *A Heart As Wide As The World. Living with Mindfulness, Wisdom and Compassion*. Boston: Shambhala.

Santorelli, S. (1999) *Heal Thyself: Lessons on Mindfulness in Medicine*. New York: Bell Tower.

Bibliography

Baer, R. A. (2003) "Mindfulness training as a clinical intervention: A conceptual and empirical review", *Clinical Psychology: Science and Practice*, 10(2): 125–143.

Barks, C., Moyne, J., Arberry, A. J. and Nicholson, R. (Translators) (1995) *The Essential Rumi*. San Francisco: Harper.

Beck, A. T., Rush, A. J., Shaw, B. F. and Emery, G. (1979) *Cognitive Therapy of Depression*. New York: Guilford Press.

Beck, C. Y. and Smith, S. (1994) *Nothing Special: Living Zen*. San Francisco: Harper.

Blacker, M. (2002) "Meditation", in M. A. Bright (ed.), *Holistic Health and Healing* (p. 105). Philadelphia: F. A. Davis Company.

Crane, R. S. and Soulsby, J. G. (2006) *Mindful Movement—Aims, Intentions and Teaching Considerations*. Bangor University, UK: unpublished handout.

Crane, R. S., Williams, J. M. G. and Soulsby, J. G. (2007) *The Three-Minute Breathing Space in MBCT—Aims, Intentions and Teaching Considerations*. Bangor University, UK: unpublished handout.

Davidson, R. J., Kabat-Zinn, J. and Schumacher, J. (2003) "Alterations in brain and immune function produced by mindfulness meditation", *Psychosomatic Medicine*, 65(4): 564–570.

Elias, D. (2006) *Mindfulness as a Process and a Practice*. Bangor University, UK: unpublished notes.

Farb, N. A. S., Segal, Z. V., Mayberg, H., Bean, J., McKeon, D.,

Fatima, Z., et al. (2007) "Attending to the present: Mindfulness meditation reveals distinct neural modes of self-reference", *Social Cognitive and Affective Neuroscience*, 2: 313–322.

Grossman, P., Niemann, M. A., Schmidt, S. and Walach, H. (2004) "Mindfulness-Based Stress Reduction and health benefits: A meta-analysis", *Journal of Psychosomatic Research*, 57(1): 35–43.

Gunaratana, B. H. (2002) *Mindfulness in Plain English*. Boston: Wisdom.

Hayes, S. C., Wilson, K. G., Gifford, E. V., Follette, V. M. and Strosahl, K. (1996) "Experiential avoidance and behavioral disorders: A functional dimensional approach to diagnosis and treatment", *Journal of Consulting and Clinical Psychology*, 64(6): 1152–1168.

Hollon, S. D., DeRubeis, R. J., Shelton, R. C., Amsterdam, J. D., Salomon, R. M., O'Reardon, J. P., et al. (2005) "Prevention of relapse following cognitive therapy vs. medications in moderate to severe depression", *Archives of General Psychiatry*, 62: 417–422.

Ingram, L. C. (2005) *A Qualitative Evaluation of Mindfulness-Based Cognitive Therapy for Oncology Outpatients*, unpublished MSc dissertation. Bath, UK: University of Bath.

James, W. (2007) *The Principles of Psychology*. New York: Cosimo Classics.

Kabat-Zinn, J. (1990) *Full Catastrophe Living: Using the Wisdom of your Body and Mind to Face Stress, Pain and Illness*. New York: Delacorte.

Kabat-Zinn, J. (1994) *Mindfulness Meditation for Everyday Life*. New York: Hyperion.

Kabat-Zinn, J. (2003) "Mindfulness-based interventions in context: Past, present and future", *Clinical Psychology Science and Practice*, 10: 144–156.

Kabat-Zinn, J. (2005) *Coming to Our Senses, Healing Ourselves and the World Through Mindfulness*. New York: Hyperion.

Kabat-Zinn, J. and Santorelli, S. (2005) *Mindfulness-Based Stress Reduction Professional Training Manual*. Worcester, MA: Center for Mindfulness, UMass.

Kenny, M. A. and Williams, J. M. G. (2007) "Treatment-resistant depressed patients show a good response to Mindfulness-Based Cognitive Therapy", *Behaviour Research and Therapy*, 45(3): 617–625.

Kingston, T., Dooley, B., Bates, A., Lawlor, E. and Malone, K. (2007) "Mindfulness-Based Cognitive Therapy for residual depressive symptoms", *Psychology and Psychotherapy: Theory, Research and Practice*, 80(2): 193–203.

Kupfer, D. J. (1991, May) "Long-term treatment of depression", *Journal of Clinical Psychiatry*, 52(Suppl.): 28–34.

Kupfer, D. J., Frank, E., Perel, J. M., Cornes, C., Mallinger, A. G., Thase, M. E., et al. (1992) "Five-year outcomes for maintenance therapies in recurrent depression", *Archives of General Psychiatry*, 49: 769–763.

Kuyken, W., Byford, S., Taylor, R. S., Watkins, E. R., Holden, E. R., White, K., et al. (in press). "Relapse prevention in recurrent depression: Mindfulness-Based Cognitive Therapy versus maintenance anti-depressant medications", *Journal of Consulting and Clinical Psychology*.

Lewis, G. (2002) *Sunbathing in the Rain: A Cheerful Book on Depression*. London: Flamingo.

Ma, S. H. and Teasdale, J. D. (2004) "Mindfulness-Based Cognitive Therapy for depression: Replication and exploration of differential relapse prevention effects", *Journal of Consulting and Clinical Psychology*, 72(1): 31–40.

Meleo-Meyer, F. (2000) *Mindful Movement Practice Tape*. Worcester, MA: Center for Mindfulness, UMass.

Murray, C. J. L. and Lopez, A. D. (1996) *The Global Burden of Disease: A Comprehensive Assessment of Mortality, Injuries and Risk Factors in 1990 and Projected to 2000*. Cambridge, MA: Harvard School of Public Health and the World Health Organization.

National Institute for Clinical Excellence (NICE) (2004) *Depression: Management in Primary and Secondary Care*, Guideline 23, p. 76.

Post, R. M. (1992) "Transduction of psychosocial stress into the neurobiology of recurrent affective disorder", *American Journal of Psychiatry*, 149: 999–1010.

Santorelli, S. (1999) *Heal Thyself: Lessons on Mindfulness in Medicine*. New York: Bell Tower.

Segal, Z. V., Williams, J. M. G. and Teasdale, J. D. (2002) *Mindfulness-Based Cognitive Therapy for Depression: A New Approach to Preventing Relapse*. New York: Guilford Press.

Surawy, C., Roberts, J. and Silver, S. (2005) "The effect of mindfulness training on mood and measures of fatigue, activity and quality of life in patients with chronic fatigue syndrome on a hospital waiting list: A series of exploratory studies", *Behavioral and Cognitive Psychotherapy*, 33: 103–109.

Teasdale, J. D. (1988) "Cognitive vulnerability to persistent depression", *Cognition and Emotion*, 2: 247–274.

Teasdale, J. D. (1999) "Metacognition, mindfulness and the modification of mood disorders", *Behavioural and Cognitive Psychotherapy*, 6: 146–155.

Teasdale, J. D. (2006) "Mindfulness-Based Cognitive Therapy for depression", in D. K. Nauriyal, M. S. Drummond and Y. B. Lal (eds), *Buddhist Thought and Applied Psychological Research: Transcending the Boundaries* (pp. 414–430). London: Routledge Curzon.

Teasdale, J. D., Segal, Z. V. and Williams, J. M. G. (1995) "How does cognitive therapy prevent depressive relapse and why should attentional control (mindfulness) training help?" *Behavioral Research and Therapy*, 33: 25–39.

Teasdale, J. D., Segal, Z. V. and Williams, J. M. G. (2000) "Prevention of relapse/recurrence in major depression by Mindfulness-Based Cognitive Therapy", *Journal of Consulting and Clinical Psychology*, 68(4): 615–623.

Teasdale, J. D., Segal, Z. V. and Williams, J. M. G. (2003) "Mindfulness training and problem formulation", *Clinical Psychology: Science and Practice*, 10(2): 157–160.

Welwood, J. (2000) *Toward a Psychology of Awakening, Buddhism, Psychotherapy and the Path of Personal and Spiritual Transformation*. Boston: Shambhala.

Williams, J. M. G. (2008, April) "Mood, memory and mindfulness", Keynote Address to 6th Annual Conference for Center for Mindfulness in Medicine, Health Care, and Society, University of Massachusetts Medical School.

Williams, J. M. G., Alatiq, Y., Crane, C., Barnhofer, T., Fennell, M. J. V., Duggan, D. S., et al. (2007a) "Mindfulness-Based Cognitive Therapy (MBCT) in bipolar disorder: Preliminary evaluation of immediate effects on between-episode functioning", *Journal of Affective Disorders*, 107(1–3): 275–279.

Williams, J. M. G., Crane, R. S. and Soulsby, J. G. (2006a) *The Eating a Raisin Practice—Aims, Intentions and Teaching Considerations*; *The Body Scan—Aims, Intentions and Teaching Considerations*; and "*Sitting Meditation—Aims, Intentions and Teaching Considerations*. Bangor University, UK: unpublished handouts.

Williams, J. M. G., Duggan, D., Crane, C. and Fennell, M. J. V. (2006b) "Mindfulness-Based Cognitive Therapy for prevention of recurrence of suicidal behaviour", *Journal of Clinical Psychology*, 62: 201–210.

Williams, J. M. G., Teasdale, J. D., Segal, Z. V. and Kabat-Zinn, J. (2007b) *The Mindful Way Through Depression: Freeing Yourself From Chronic Unhappiness*. New York: Guilford Press.

Index